Fiscal measures for poverty alleviation in the United States

FISCAL MEASURES FOR POVERTY ALLEVIATION IN THE UNITED STATES

David Hsieh

International Labour Office Geneva

ISBN 92-2-102107-6

First published 1979

The designations employed in ILO publications, which are in conformity with United Nations practice, and the presentation of material therein do not imply the expression of any opinion whatsoever on the part of the International Labour Office concerning the legal status of any country or territory or of its authorities, or concerning the delimitation of its frontiers.
The responsibility for opinions expressed in signed articles, studies and other contributions rests solely with their authors, and publication does not constitute an endorsement by the International Labour Office of the opinions expressed in them.

ILO publications can be obtained through major booksellers or ILO local offices in many countries, or direct from ILO Publications, International Labour Office, CH-1211 Geneva 22, Switzerland. A catalogue or list of new publications will be sent free of charge from the above address.

Printed by the International Labour Office, Geneva, Switzerland

Table of contents

Pages

Introduction

Elimination of poverty is a leading social issue in both developed and developing countries. A commonly suggested approach to the poverty problem in both groups of countries is to establish a minimum living standard or a poverty line (or lines) and to devise policies to bring the population living below the defined standard up to and above this standard.

The present study is one of poverty policy and programmes in the United States. It may be recalled that in the early 1960s there was surging dissatisfaction among the disadvantaged and underprivileged population in the United States manifesting itself in vigorous protests against inequality of treatment, the most notable protest being the rise of the civil rights movement. To attenuate growing social discontent and unrest, the Johnson Administration initiated a number of major social reform measures, mostly in 1964 and 1965, under the label of the "Great Society Programmes". One of the goals of the Great Society was the elimination of poverty which was put forth strongly in the declaration of "unconditional war on poverty in America" by President Johnson in his State of Union Message in January 1964.

The war-on-poverty declared by President Johnson was characterised by a mixture of two approaches. The first was an innovative grass-roots approach to correcting the causes of poverty at the local level. This approach comprised a variety of federal-financed programmes, in particular, those for developing the earning capacity of the poor through education and training and for improving the environment and social and legal services in low-income areas through community action with active participation of the poor. These programmes were embodied in the Economic Opportunity Act of 1964 and administered by the Office of Economic Opportunity established by the Act. The second was an income transfer approach designed to alleviate the suffering of the existing poor by providing them with public transfer payments in cash and/or in kind. Unlike the first, this second approach had long been put into practice especially since the enactment of social security legislation in 1934 and was reflected regularly in public budgets under social insurance and social assistance programmes.

The grass-roots approach described above played a major role in the early years of the war-on-poverty. But its effects on poverty would be felt only after a long lapse of time. Furthermore, several programmes under this approach did not meet with distinct success for various reasons.[1] Hence, in the subsequent years a greater emphasis was placed on the income transfer approach. Though it did not root out the causes of poverty, the latter approach did make a direct and immediate impact on reducing the income poverty of the poor.

---

[1] Cf. Institute for Research on Poverty, University of Wisconsin - Madison: A Decade of Federal Antipoverty Program: Achievements, Failures and Lessons, edited by Robert H. Haveman (Academic Press, New York, San Francisco, London, Mar. 1977).

In the present study of poverty policy in the United States the focus is on the income transfer approach. The main content of this study is indicated briefly below.

Chapter 1 describes the magnitude, trends and profile of poverty in the United States. It explains first the official poverty standard or poverty line in use. Attention is drawn to the inadequacies of this standard and the desirability of adopting a higher absolute standard or a relative poverty standard. The distinction between pre-transfer and post-transfer poverty and the shortcomings of existing annual data on pre-transfer poverty are stressed.

In regard to the magnitude of poverty some illustrations are given of the increases in the magnitude of post-transfer poverty if the poverty standard is raised from the official poverty line to some higher absolute standards suggested by other writers. From some recent studies findings on the high pre-transfer poverty incidence by the official poverty line are also shown.

With respect to the movement of poverty trends, where data were available, pre-transfer poverty and post-transfer poverty are estimated separately. Of particular significance is the marked difference found between the post-transfer poverty trend measured by the official poverty line and that measured by a commonly used relative poverty standard. For the long-term declining trend in post-transfer poverty between 1960 and 1975 an explanation is offered in terms of the combination of a rising trend in public income transfers and a saucer-shaped trend in pre-transfer poverty over the period under review.

The profile of poverty analysed refers chiefly to post-transfer poverty based on money income data for 1975. The lack of detailed data on distribution of in-kind public transfers among various subgroups of the poverty population may cause some distortion in the poverty profile presented. None the less, the analysis made has brought to light the wide differences in post-transfer poverty incidence among certain subgroups, in particular, the much higher incidence for non-whites than for whites, for female-headed families than for male-headed families, for unrelated individuals living together than for persons living in families, and in the South rather than in the rest of the country. A further examination is made of the association of high post-transfer poverty incidence with certain characteristics of the poor families. From this examination emerge several important findings.

Chapter 2 is devoted to a systematic review of the fiscal expenditures on poverty alleviation and detailed analysis of the effects of public income transfers on poverty alleviation. The first section presents an overview of the public social welfare expenditures - federal, state and local - over the period 1960-75, pointing out, inter alia, the enormous absolute and relative expansion of these expenditures in public budget, the rapid growth in the proportion of these expenditures allotted to income maintenance compared with those allotted to human investment, and, within income maintenance expenditures, the predominance of specific programmes.

The second section presents a substantive review of six income maintenance programmes: old-age, survivor, disability insurance (OASDI), unemployment insurance, aid to families with dependent children, general assistance, medicaid and food stamps. In addition, public employment is discussed. For each programme the coverage, eligibility requirements, the amount of contribution required, where applicable, benefit levels (compared with the official poverty line), and its limitations and drawbacks are analysed.

The third section, as a complement to Chapter 1, enters a further discussion of the extent to which the public income maintenance programmes have reduced poverty in the country, based on data provided in some recent studies. Here emphasis is more on the effects of different programmes and on different subgroups of the poverty population. In both respects great differences are found.

The fourth section brings together systematically the main drawbacks previously discussed separately with respect to various individual programmes. This critical assessment points to the immediate need for reforming the existing income maintenance system. In this connection an analysis is made of President Carter's welfare reform plan proposed in August 1977.

Chapter 3 steps beyond the confines of the income maintenance system to examine two major drawbacks of US tax systems (inclusive of federal, state and local taxes) from the point of view of poverty alleviation and income redistribution. These are the heavy taxation of the poor and favourable treatment of the rich. These two drawbacks combined to reduce further the inadequate disposable incomes of the poor and, contrariwise, boost larger disposable incomes of the rich. The main elements contributing to each drawback are reviewed at some length. The analysis has shown that the enormous tax benefits reaped by the upper income groups were likely to exceed the public transfer payments received by the lowest income groups, and that the transfer payments received by the lowest income groups were, to a large extent, offset by the heavy taxes they paid. These irrationalities point equally to the need for a reform of the tax system, in addition to the need for reforming the welfare system. The chapter reviews some proposals for federal tax reform as well as a number of negative income tax plans designed especially to deal with the poverty problem.

In concluding this study, Chapter 4 restates some of the important findings on poverty alleviation from the study and makes a few observations on the future. First, it repeats the explanation offered earlier of the long-term declining trend in post-transfer poverty between 1960 and 1975 in terms of the combination of a rapidly rising trend in public income transfers and a saucer-shaped trend in pre-transfer poverty. Second, the relatively high pre-transfer poverty incidence in the United States is stressed, and some of its immediate causes are indicated. Third, while remedies for pre-transfer poverty are beyond the scope of this study, the chapter provides a summary of the shortcomings of the existing income transfer or maintenance system and, in particular, those found in the welfare system (or the means-tested income assistance component) within the over-all system. Finally, in regard to future policy, a range of options for reforming the welfare system have been put forward. In this chapter several of these options are compared and commented upon from the point of view of their effectiveness in rectifying the serious shortcomings contained in the existing system.

Chapter 1

Poverty in the United States

Poverty is more than the lack of income or a problem of economic insufficiency. Its economic dimension is causally related to its social and political dimensions. In the social sphere poverty has been attributed largely to social stratification. There are theories emphasising that the poor as the lowest social class suffer from intergenerational immobility as well as occupational immobility due to stratified labour markets. Their bargaining strength is weak vis-à-vis their employers. More importantly, they are known to have relatively little political power to better their own lot. In the political process the decision making of direct concern to the poor is generally influenced by the interests of upper and middle social classes. These other dimensions need to be carefully studied for a deeper understanding of poverty in the United States as in most other countries.

In this chapter the focus is placed on the economic dimension of poverty and, in particular, on income inadequacy or physical deprivation of the population. The degree of income poverty depends much on the definition of poverty adopted. Accordingly, the chapter begins with a discussion of the official poverty line used in the United States, some of the criticisms and certain alternative definitions. This is followed by a description of the magnitude and the profile of poverty in the United States based on the official definition. Wherever data permit, data based on alternative definitions are presented for comparison. As regards its magnitude, the extent of poverty reduction attributed to public cash transfers given in this chapter deserves particular attention from the fiscal point of view.

The official poverty line

For carrying out the war-on-poverty declared by President Johnson in 1964 mentioned previously, the need was immediately felt for a clear notion of the nature and extent of poverty prevailing in the country. Attempts were therefore made towards developing an official definition of poverty amenable to measurement.

The first attempt in this direction can be found in the 1964 annual report of the President's Council of Economic Advisers which stated:[1]

> By the poor we mean those who are not now maintaining a decent standard of living - those whose basic needs exceed their means to satisfy them.

---

[1] Economic Report of the President to the Congress, January 1964, Together With the Annual Report of the Council of Economic Advisers (Washington, D.C., Government Printing Office, 1964), p. 57.

Guided by this conception, which begs many questions, the Council used as a working definition an annual family money income of $3,000 in 1962 prices (before taxes) for a family of four as a boundary of poverty. By this crude measure 33 to 35 million persons were found to live at or below the boundary of poverty in 1962 or nearly 20 per cent of the population.[1]

The definition in use

In 1965 a more refined official definition of poverty was announced as a result of further research done in the Social Security Administration (SSA).[2] It takes the form of a matrix of the minimum total money income requirements established by the Federal Government for families of different sizes (including unrelated individuals) and of different age and sex composition, taking into account farm or non-farm residence. These minimum income requirements rest on a fixed minimum level of consumption below which people are considered as living in poverty. Hence, the minimum money income requirements are designated as poverty lines or low-income levels.

Methodologically, this elaborate definition, which has been in use ever since, is based on a "semi-basket approach". For each different type of family and unrelated individual, the minimum total money income required, or the poverty line income, was obtained by multiplying the corresponding minimum cost of maintaining nutritional adequacy by a ratio of income to food expenditure (i.e. the reciprocal of an Engel coefficient). The size of the poverty line income thus depends on the numerical value chosen for these two components.

---

[1] ibid., p. 59.

[2] For a detailed explanation of the methodology used in developing this definition see Mollie Orshansky: "Counting the Poor: Another Look at the Poverty Profile", in <u>Social Security Bulletin</u> (Washington, D.C., US Department of Health, Education and Welfare), Vol. 28, No. 1, Jan. 1965, pp. 3-29.

For determining the minimum cost of nutritional adequacy, the SSA faced a choice between the low-cost food plan and the economy food plan developed by the Department of Agriculture.[1] The low-cost food plan, adapted to the food pattern of the lowest third of the income range, had been used by welfare agencies as a basis for food allotments for needy families. The economy food plan costs about 20-25 per cent less than the low-cost food plan and is considered acceptable only for "temporary and emergency use when funds are low".[2] The SSA chose the cost of the economy food plan, at January 1964 prices, as the point of departure for computing the minimum total income requirement for families of different types.[3]

As regards the income-food expenditure relationship, the SSA used the Engel coefficients (i.e. the ratio of food expenditure to income) from the 1955 Department of Agriculture Survey as the basis for computation. The coefficients adopted were 33 per cent

---

[1] The cost per month of US Department of Agriculture's Economy Food Plan and Low-cost Food Plan (as of December) for selected family types in 1972, 1973, 1974 and 1975 are shown below:

Family members	1972		1973		1974		1975	
	Economy plan	Low-cost plan	Economy plan	Low-cost plan	Economy plan	Low-cost plan	Economy plan	Low-cost plan
Women 35-55 ys	$33.50	$41.90	$40.90	$51.10				
Couple 55-75 ys	56.40	70.50	68.90	86.00				
Parents 20-35 ys + 2 preschool chldn	99.80	124.90	122.40	152.90				
Parents 20-35 ys + 2 elem school chldn	115.90	145.00	142.10	177.50				
Parents 35-55 ys + 2 preschool + 2 elem school chldn + 2 tngrs	192.60	240.90	236.10	294.90				

Source: US Bureau of the Census: Statistical Abstract of the United States: 1974 (Washington, D.C.), p. 91.

[2] Mollie Orshansky, loc. cit., p. 6.

[3] This paragraph is based on Mollie Orshansky, loc. cit., pp. 5-6.

for a family of three or more persons and 27 per cent for a family of two members, the reciprocal of these coefficients being respectively 3 and 3.7. For an unrelated individual living alone the income cut-off was assumed at 80 per cent of the minimum money income requirement for a couple.[1]

Since the poverty line income covered by the definition is limited to money income, a rate of deduction has been applied to the computation of poverty line incomes for farm families primarily on the ground that the food they consume can be met in part from their own production. The rate of deduction has been revised successively downwards from 40 per cent less than the corresponding non-farm income levels to 15 per cent in 1969.[2]

With the methodology described above the SSA developed a matrix of poverty income lines for 1963 which are adjusted each year for changes in the cost of living.[3] As an illustration, table 1 presents the average poverty line income for a non-farm family of four persons together with the changes in the Consumer Price Index (1963 = 100) from 1959 to 1975;[4] table 2 gives the weighted average poverty line incomes in 1975 by size of family and sex of head and by farm or non-farm residence.

The concept of income used for measuring poverty by the official poverty definition is money income for the year before tax and after public cash transfers. Though it has serious shortcomings, this concept of income has been chosen because it accords with the concept used for the income data collected annually by the

---

[1] Mollie Orshansky, loc. cit., pp. 7-9.

[2] See US Bureau of the Census: Characteristics of the Low-Income Population: 1973, op. cit., pp. 159-160.

[3] The matrix is arranged according to family size (from one person (i.e. unrelated individual) to 7 or more persons) and cross-classified by (a) presence and number of related children under 18 years of age (from none to 6 or more children), (b) sex of head of family, and (c) farm or non-farm residence. Unrelated individuals and two-person families are further differentiated by age of head (under 65 years and 65 years and over). (See Mollie Orshansky, loc. cit., table F, p. 29.)

[4] Prior to 1969 adjustment was based on the changes in the price of foods in the economy plan. Since 1969 the basis for adjustment has been changed to the Consumer Price Index. However, neither method has proved to be satisfactory because of the differences in relative compostion between the budget of poor families and the family budget used for the construction of the Consumer Price Index. For instance, during 1973 and 1974 when food prices rose markedly faster than the Consumer Price Index, the use of the Consumer Price Index led to a substantial underestimation of the number of persons living below the poverty line.

Bureau of the Census in the Current Population Survey.[1] On the basis of the income data thus collected, the Census Bureau, by using the official poverty lines as a yardstick, compiles and publishes each year detailed official statistics on poverty status of the population.

Thus two main features of the Census Bureau's poverty statistics need to be indicated at the outset. First, these poverty statistics refer to post-transfer poverty as distinct from pre-transfer poverty which will also be considered in this study. Second, the magnitude of post-transfer poverty derived from these statistics has been overestimated because the income concept used includes public cash transfers but excludes public in-kind transfers.

Criticisms and alternatives

Notwithstanding the meticulousness of its construction, the official definition of poverty has been subjected to criticisms on various grounds. Two major criticisms are worthy of careful consideration. These are the meagreness of the poverty-line incomes as officially defined; and the inadequacy of the concept of absolute poverty underlying the offical definition, i.e. the need for some relativity in the poverty standard.

(a) The meagreness of the official poverty line incomes

The official poverty line incomes established in terms of "minimum needs" has been criticised as much too low in relation to the average American standard of living. These needs are regarded as no more than a "minimum subsistence standard".[2]

---

[1] The following provides a fuller explanation of the income concept used: "Data on income collected in the Current Population Survey are limited to money income received before payments for personal income taxes, social security, union dues, medicare deductions, etc. Money income is the sum of the amounts received from earnings; social security and public assistance payments; dividends, interest and rent; unemployment and workmen's compensation; government and private employee pensions, and other periodic income. (Certain money receipts such as capital gains are not included.)" (US Department of Commerce, Bureau of the Census: Current Population Reports, Consumer Income: Series P-60, No. 98: *Characteristics of the Low-Income Population: 1973* (Jan. 1975, Washington, D.C.) p. 157.) It should be mentioned that private cash transfers such as alimony and regular contributions from persons not living in the household are also included. (See ibid., p. 156.)

[2] *Manpower Report of the President, 1970* (Washington, D.C.), p. 120.

Table 1

The Average Poverty Income Line for a Non-Farm Family of Four and the Consumer Price Index, 1959-1975

Year	Consumer Price Index (1963=100)	Average Poverty Income Line for a non-farm family of four (in current dollars)
1959	95.2	2 973
1960	96.7	3 022
1961	97.7	3 054
1962	98.8	3 089
1963	100.0	3 128
1964	101.3	3 169
1965	103.1	3 223
1966	106.0	3 317
1967	109.1	3 410
1968	113.6	3 553
1969	119.7	3 743
1970	126.8	3 968
1971	132.3	4 137
1972	136.6	4 275
1973	145.1	4 540
1974	161.1	5 038
1975	175.9	5 500

Source: Figures for 1959 to 1973 are from the US Bureau of the Census: *Characteristics of the Low-Income Population: 1973*, op. cit. p. 160. Figures for 1974 and 1975 are from the US Bureau of Statistics: Current Population Reports; Consumer Income, Series P-60, No. 103: *Money Income and Poverty Status of Families and Persons in the United States: 1975 and 1974 Revisions (Advance Report)* (issued Sep. 1976, Washington,D.C.), p. 45. For 1974 and 1975 the Consumer Price Index with 1963 as base year was computed from Consumer Price Index for 1973 and the poverty income lines for 1973, 1974 and 1975 given in table 1.

Table 2

Weighted Average Poverty-Income Lines in 1975 by Size of Family, Sex of Head and by Farm and Non-Farm Residence (in current dollars)

Size of family unit	Total	Non-farm			Farm		
		Total	Male Head(1)	Female Head(1)	Total	Male Head(1)	Female Head(1)
1 person (unrelated individual)	2 717	2 724	2 851	2 635	2 305	2 396	2 224
14 to 64 years	2 791	2 797	2 902	2 685	2 396	2 466	2 282
65 years and over	2 572	2 581	2 608	2 574	2 196	2 216	2 187
2 persons	3 485	3 506	3 515	3 460	2 955	2 963	2 834
head 14 to 64 years	3 599	3 617	3 636	3 530	3 079	3 086	2 933
" 65 years and over	3 232	3 257	3 260	3 237	2 772	2 772	2 770
3 persons	4 269	4 293	4 317	4 175	3 643	3 652	3 480
4 persons	5 469	5 500	5 502	5 473	4 695	4 697	4 616
5 persons	6 463	6 499	6 504	6 434	5 552	5 552	5 595
6 persons	7 272	7 316	7 322	7 270	6 224	6 230	6 105
7 persons or more	8 939	9 022	9 056	8 818	7 639	7 639	7 647

Source: US Bureau of the Census: Current Population Reports, Consumer Income, Series P-60, No. 103: Money Income and Poverty Status of Families and Persons in the United States: 1975 and 1974 Revisions (Advance Report) (issued Sep. 1976, Washington, D.C.), p. 33.

(1) For one person (i.e., unrelated individual), sex of the individual.

Much of this criticism is levelled against the use of the economy food plan. As indicated earlier, the economy food plan is designed only for temporary and emergency use. The diet drawn up by the plan is considered "nutritionally inadequate for an extended period of time".[1] Further, the cost calculation for this plan is based on the most economic possible food basket. This demands extraordinary skills in marketing and food preparation which few housewives possess. Besides, poor families often purchase the same kind of food as richer families but at higher prices because of their inability to make bulk purchases. Regarding the computed cost of the economy food plan, "studies show that most families that spend this little do not select foods which would comprise an adequate diet".[2]

One investigation has shown that, living within the family budget at the poverty line, the poor family must do without many of the things which families with an average income consider to be "necessities" - a car, an occasional dessert after meals, rugs, a bed for each family member, school supplies, or an occasional movie. Nothing can be budgeted for medical care or insurance.[3]

In money terms the meagreness of the official poverty definition can be seen by comparing the official poverty-line income for a non-farm family of four to the median family income, the per capita personal income and the average weekly earnings. As is shown in table 3, in 1973, the year before the 1974-75 recession, the official poverty definition amounted to only 38 per cent of the median income of all families, the latter based on the same pre-tax, post-transfer money income concept as used in the official poverty definition.[4] On a per capita basis it was less than one-quarter (23 per cent) of the per capita personal income of the whole population which was also post-transfer but based on a different income concept.[5] When the annual official poverty-line income for a non-farm family of four was converted into weekly income, it amounted to

---

[1] View expressed by Frederick Parella, co-author (with Mariellen Procopio) of a report on poverty prepared for an anti-poverty agency of the US Catholic Conference (released in 1975) as reported in International Herald Tribune (Paris), 26 Dec. 1975, p. 3.

[2] US Bureau of the Census: Statistical Abstract of the United States: 1974 (Washington, D.C.) p. 91.

[3] Extract from Poverty Amid Plenty: The American Paradox, Report of the President's Commission on Income Maintenance Programme (Washington, D.C., 1969), reproduced in Theodore R. Marmor (ed.): Poverty Policy: A Compendium of Cash Transfer Proposals (Chicago, Aldine-Atherton, 1971), p. 5.

[4] Estimates of median family incomes were derived from the same income data collected by the Bureau of the Census in the Current Population Survey.

[5] Personal income in the US usage includes government transfer payments and various types of non-money income (e.g. wages received in kind, the net rental value of owner-occupied homes, the value of food and fuel produced and consumed on farms). It includes personal income taxes but excludes employee contribution for social security. The personal income series was prepared by the Bureau of Economic Analysis of the US Department of Commerce.

Table 3

Average Poverty line Income for a Non-farm Family of Four compared with OECD Poverty Standard, Per Capita Personal Income, Median Income of All Families and Gross Average Weekly Earnings of Private Non-agricultural Workers (in current dollars)

	Poverty line income for a non-farm family of four (a)	Per capita disposable personal income (b)	OECD poverty standard (1.45 times(b)) (c)	(a) as per cent of (c) (d)	Per capita personal income (e)	(a)/4 as per cent of (e) (f)	Median income of all families (g)	(a) as per cent of (g) (h)	gross average weekly earnings of private non-agricultural workers[1] (i)	(a)/52 as per cent of (i) (j)
1960	$3 022	$1 934	$2 804	107.8%	$2 219	34%	$5 620	54%	$80.67	72%
1965	3 223	2 430	3 523	91.5	2 773	29	6 956	46	95.06	65
1970	3 968	3 348	4 855	81.7	3 945	25	9 867	40	119.46	64
1971	4 137	3 588	5 203	79.5	4 171	25	10 285	40	127.28	62
1972	4 275	3 837	5 564	76.8	4 497	24	11 116	38	136.16	60
1973	4 540	4 292	6 223	73.0	5 011	23	12 051	38	145.43	60
1974	5 038	4 642	6 731	74.8	5 449	23	12 902	39	154.45	62
1975	5 500	5 040	7 308	75.3	5 832	24	13 719	40	163.89	65

Source: Figures for poverty line income were from the sources given in table 1. Figures for per capita disposable income from Economic Report of the President Transmitted to the Congress January 1976 (Washington 1976), p.191; per capita personal income for 1960 to 1972 from Statistical Abstract of the United States: 1974, op. cit., p. 382; per capita personal income for 1973 to 1975 computed from statistics on personal income and population given in Economic Report of the President Transmitted to the Congress January 1976, op. cit., p. 188 and p. 191; median income for all families for 1960 to 1975 from US Bureau of the Census: Money Income and Poverty Status of Families and Persons in the United States: 1975 and 1974 Revisions (Advance Report), op. cit., p. 15; gross average weekly earnings of private non-agricultural workers were from US Department of Labour: Monthly Labour Review, Vol. 98, No. 5, May 1975, p. 98 and Vol. 99, No. 6, June 1976, p. 90.

[1] Figures refer to earnings (including social security and Federal Income Taxes) of production or non-supervisory workers on private non-agricultural payrolls.

60 per cent of the average gross weekly earnings of production of non-supervisory workers in the private non-agricultural sector.[1] In 1974 and 1975 when the income and earnings used for comparison decreased in real terms, the differences were correspondingly reduced.

One reason offered for the meagreness of the poverty-line incomes under the official definition was that in constructing the official poverty lines technical decisions which could affect the extent of poverty were influenced by political acceptability. It was "the political views and realities which provide the framework for professional judgements".[2]

Nevertheless, it has been contended that with its enormous productive capacity the United States could well afford to adopt a standard of absolute poverty substantially higher than the official poverty line. In this connection attention may be drawn to the following alternative standards:

1. Poverty standards set at 25 per cent or 50 per cent above the official poverty line. The reports on Poverty Status of the Population published by the Bureau of the Census include also the number and characteristics of population below these higher standards.

2. The lower urban budget for a family of four published regularly by the US Bureau of Labour Statistics (BLS) together with the intermediate urban budget and the higher urban budget.[3]

---

[1] Gross weekly earnings include premium pay for overtime or late shift work as well as personal income taxes and employee's contribution for social security, but excludes irregular bonuses and other special payments.

[2] Martin Rein: "Problems in the definition and measurement of Poverty", in Peter Townsend (ed.): _The Concept of Poverty: Working Papers on Methods of Investigation and Life-Styles of the Poor in Different Countries_ (Heinemann, London, 1970), p. 56. For a similar view on the official definition of poverty and its political acceptability, see Robert D. Plotnik and Felicity Skidmore: _Progress Against Poverty: A Review of the 1964-1974 Decade_ (Institute for Research on Poverty, University of Wisconsin, Academic Press, New York, San Francisco, London, 1975), pp. 36-37.

[3] The BLS lower urban budget is not intended to represent a minimum or subsistence standard. The costs of the three BLS annual urban budgets in current dollars (as of autumn) in 1972, 1973 and 1974 are as follows:

Urban budgets for a 4-person family (in current dollars)

	Lower budget	Intermediate budget	Higher budget
Autumn 1972	7 386	11 446	16 558
Autumn 1973	8 181	12 626	18 201
Autumn 1974	9 198	14 333	20 777

Source: US Bureau of the Census: _Statistical Abstract of the United States_: 1975 (Washington, D.C., 1976), p. 428.

3. The poverty standard used by the Organisation for Economic Co-operation and Development (OECD) which consists of a set of ratios of family income to per capita disposable income as a basis for setting poverty standards for families of different sizes. These ratios are the averages of the corresponding ratios of poverty-line income to per capita disposable income in six developed countries including the United States.[1] Disposable income as defined by OECD is post-tax and post-transfer (post-benefit) money income.[2]

A comparison is made of the three income levels (100, 125, 150 per cent) relating to the official poverty line for a 4-person non-farm family with the OECD poverty standard and the BLS lower urban budget both for a 4-person family in 1973, 1974 and 1975. The OECD standard is set for measuring post-transfer relative poverty but can also be treated as a standard for post-transfer absolute poverty in any given year. For a 4-person family it is set at 145 per cent of per capita disposable income. As indicated above, per capita disposable income as defined by OECD is in terms of post-tax and post-transfer money income. In the United States the statistics on per capita disposable personal income are post-tax and post-transfer but, as already noted, include certain types of non-money income. The OECD standard computed from these statistics is therefore expected to be higher than would be obtained strictly on a money basis. Allowing for this difference, in 1975 the official poverty-line income for a 4-person non-farm family was approximately one-quarter below the OECD standard as shown in table 3. To conform with the OECD standard thus computed, the official poverty line would need to be raised from $5,500 to $7,308.

The gap between the official poverty line and the BLS lower urban budget was much larger. At the living costs prevailing in autumn in 1974 the BLS lower urban budget amounted to $9,198. To move up to this level the official poverty-line income, which was $5,038 in 1974, would require an increase of 83 per cent. Some

---

[1] The other five developed countries included are Australia, Canada, United Kingdom, Belgium and Ireland. The ratios of family income to per capita disposable income are thus derived and used by OECD for setting poverty standards and are given below:

Size of family	Poverty level income as per cent of per capita disposable income
1 person	66.2/3
2 persons	100
3 persons	125
4 persons	145
5 persons	160

Source: Organisation for Economic Co-operation and Development (OECD): Public Expenditure on Income Maintenance Programmes (Paris, July 1976), p. 66.

[2] ibid., p. 66.

writers have taken the view that "as a budget reflecting the price of a basket of goods necessary to ensure some minimum sense of social satisfaction in our urban environment, the BLS 'low-level' budget is a vast, albeit not a final, improvement on the 'official poverty' budget".[1]

As can be seen from table, 4, between the offical poverty line and the BLS lower urban budget there is a fairly wide range of suggested income levels from which a standard for absolute poverty may be chosen. Obviously, a higher poverty standard means that a larger number of persons would be counted as poor, and is also expected to entail changes in the composition of the poverty population.[2] However, the larger the size of poverty and the greater the changes in its composition revealed by the definition used, the more far-reaching policy measures and more public expenditures would be needed for its elimination.

(b) The need for a relative poverty standard

Conceptually, a more serious criticism of the offical definition has to do with the concept of absolute poverty underlying this definition. As economic growth proceeds and the level of real incomes rises, the official poverty income lines are bound to fall increasingly behind the rising average personal income. This is clearly shown in table 3. Between 1960 and 1973, the year before the 1974-75 severe recession, the income per head of a non-farm family of four at the poverty line as a percentage of average personal income per head of the whole population fell from 34 per cent to 23 per cent. As a percentage of the median income of all families, the poverty-line income for a family of four fell from 54 to 38 per cent. In both instances the ratio decreased by no less than 30 per cent. Over this 13-year period the population living within and below the fixed official poverty budget had been drifting further and further away from the mainstream of the American community.

---

[1] T. Vietorisz, R. Mier and J. Giblin: "Sub-employment: exclusion and inadequacy indexes", in US Department of Labour Statistics: Monthly Labour Review, Vol. 98, No. 5, May 1975, p. 11.

[2] On the question of the composition of the poverty population, a recent official report on the measure of poverty has brought out the following findings: "Increasing the poverty lines results in a poverty population with proportionately more whites than at present more working poor, an increased proportion of families with a male rather than a female head, and slightly higher concentrations of the elderly, and slightly lower concentrations of children. It also causes a relative shift in the proportionate share of the poor population from the Southern to other States and from less populated to more populated States." The Executive Summary of The Measure of Poverty, A report to Congress As Mandated by the Education Amendments of 1974 (US Department of Health, Education and Welfare, 1976), reproduced in US Department of Health, Education and Welfare: Social Security Administration. Social Security Bulletin (Washington, D.C., Vol. 39, No. 9, Sep. 1976), p. 36.

Table 4

The Official Poverty line Income of a 4-Person Non-farm Family and 25 per cent and 50 per cent above as per cent of the corresponding OECD Poverty Standard and BLS Lower Urban Budget: 1973, 1974 and 1975
(in current dollars)

		Official poverty line income			125 per cent of official poverty line income			150 per cent of official poverty line income		
		1973	1974	1975	1973	1974	1975	1973	1974	1975
	Amount	$4 540	$5 038	$5 500	$5 675	$6 298	$6 875	$6 810	$7 557	$8 250
OECD Poverty Standard		%	%	%	%	%	%	%	%	%
1973	$6 223	73			91			109		
1974	$6 731		75			94			112	
1975	$7 308			75			94			113
BLS Lower Urban Budget										
1973	$8 181	55			69			83		
1974	$9 198		55			68			82	
1975	(a)			(a)			(a)			(a)

Source: Figures for the three income levels relating to official poverty line were taken or computed from sources given in table 1; figures for the OECD poverty standard for a 4-person family are from table 3; figures for BLS Lower Urban Budget are from US Bureau of the Census: Statistical Abstract of the United States; 1975 (Washington, D.C., 1976), p. 428.

(a) Not readily available.

The steady widening of the gap between a fixed poverty line and the average level of living over time has led to the advocacy of the concept of relative poverty. One writer maintains that "poverty in the United States in the 1960s is largely a matter of economic distance. When most Americans have a great deal, those who have much less are poor regardless of their absolute level of income."[1] In a similar vein, several other writers stated that "it is relative deprivation, a comparative position of losing out, that characterises those who are termed 'poor' in the affluent society".[2]

The concept of relative poverty likewise raises the question of definition and measurement. To those concerned merely about upward shifts in the "contemporary" living standard, all that appears necessary is to revise the level of absolute poverty in real terms periodically, say, once in a generation.[3] Many writers favour a specific definition of relative poverty focused on income distribution at the low end.

Most widely known is Victor Fuchs' proposal of one-half of the median family income (the Fuchs point): families with incomes below this point are classified as families living in poverty.[4] The choice of half of the median family income is arbitrary and perhaps not fortuitous. The extent of poverty estimated by this yardstick happens to have covered roughly the bottom 20 per cent of the population in the 1960s. The striking finding by using this relative measure is that since the end of the Second World War, relative poverty has not shown any decline in the United States. The percentage of families below the Fuchs point has remained at approximately 20 per cent of the total number of families and

---

[1] Victor R. Fuchs: "Comments on Measuring the Low-Income Population", in Lee Soltow (ed.): Six Papers on the Size Distribution of Wealth and Income, studies on Income and Wealth, No. 33 (National Bureau of Economic Research, New York, 1969), p. 198.

[2] S.M. Miller, Martin Rein, Pamela Roby and Bertrand M. Gross: "Poverty, Inequality and Conflict", in The Annuals of American Academy of Political and Social Science: Social Goals and Indicators of American Society (Philadelphia), Vol. II, Sep. 1967, p. 17.

[3] Cf. Robert J. Lampman: Ends and Means of Reducing Income Poverty (Institute for Research on Poverty (Monograph Series), University of Wisconsin, Markham Publishing Company, Chicago, 1971), p. 53.

[4] Victor R. Fuchs: "Commenting on Measuring the Low-Income Population", in Lee Soltow (ed.): Six Papers on the Size Distribution of Wealth and Income (National Bureau of Economic Research, New York, 1969), pp. 108-202.

estimates foresaw "a continued rough constancy through 1980".[1] As can be inferred from the income data from which the median family income was estimated, the size of relative poverty thus obtained refers to post-transfer poverty.

One variant of the Fuchs point suggested by Bruno Stein is to take half of the income of the median family headed by a year-round full-time worker as the relative measure, the latter considered as a more relevant group with whom people compare themselves. By this measure, the poverty income line would be substantially higher than that based on the Fuchs point, though judging by the same source of income data used, it refers similarly to post-transfer relative poverty.[2]

A different relative measure recently used by Plotnick and Skidmore is to define the relative poor as those with welfare ratios below 0.44 of the median ratio. For each family a "welfare ratio" was calculated by dividing each family's current cash income[3] by the official poverty line, yielding the fraction by which the family's income exceeded or fell below the official poverty line. Families were then ranked according to the welfare ratio thus obtained. The fraction 0.44 of the median welfare ratio was selected as the measure of relative poverty because in the base year of 1965, which the authors used, the median welfare ratio was 2.25. Thus, the families classified as the poor by the official poverty line in 1965 necessarily had a welfare ratio less than 0.44 of the median (that is 1/2.25 of the median). The use of this particular relative measure renders it possible to trace

---

[1] Extract from Poverty Amid Plenty: the American Paradox: Report of the President's Commission on Income Maintenance Programs (Washington, 1969), reproduced in Theodore R. Marmor (ed.) Poverty Policy, A Compendium of Cash Transfer Proposals (Chicago, Aldine-Atherton, 1971), p. 5.

[2] The income of the median family headed by a year-round full-time worker was estimated from the income data collected in the Current Population Survey. Stein illustrated that measured by his variant of the Fuchs point the poverty income line in March 1969 was $5,057 compared to $4,316 measured by the Fuchs point. See Bruno Stein: One Relief: The Economics of Poverty and Public Welfare (Basic Books Inc., New York, London, 1971), p. 12.

[3] Plotnick and Skidmore have measured relative poverty both before and after public cash transfers (pre-transfer and post-transfer). For post-transfer relative poverty, the income concept they used is the same pre-tax, post-transfer money income concept as used in the official poverty definition. For pre-transfer relative poverty, the income concept used is pre-tax money income before public cash transfers (i.e. the sum of wages, salaries, property income and private transfers). The same income concepts were applied to their measurement of post-transfer and pre-transfer absolute poverty. (See Robert D. Plotnick and Felicity Skidmore: Progress Against Poverty: A Review of the 1964-1974 Decade, op. cit., pp. 42-43, p. 75, note 1, p. 112 and p. 132, note 4.)

changes over time in the poverty population by either an absolute or relative standard against exactly the same basis.[1] Conceptually, by linking relative poverty to absolute poverty, this measure differs greatly from the Fuchs point, but it has many advantages.

Lastly, the OECD standard referred to earlier is likewise a relative poverty standard linked with absolute poverty in its construction. It is designed for inter-temporal as well as inter-country comparison. The distinction it makes between families of different size facilitates its use for operational purposes.

For policies of income redistribution the relative poverty standards considered above, by concentrating on the low end of the income scale, provide, in fact, only a partial indication of the state of income inequalities in the country. Some writers have proposed the use of the Gini coefficient as a statistical tool for setting targets for reducing relative poverty. For instance, David M. Gordon has suggested reducing the Gini coefficient of income inequality for families and unrelated individuals in the United States from 0.406 in 1968 to a fractional minimum somewhere between 0.100 and 0.150 within a generation (or 25 years), or by at least 0.010 point per year.[2] A decrease in the Gini coefficient, which reflects a diminution of over-all inequality in income distribution, however, gives no indication of the extent to which a reduction in relative poverty has been brought about by redistributing income from upper income groups to the bottom income group. For the latter purpose, some other statistical measures need to be developed. For example, a measure of relative poverty may be complemented by a measure of relative affluence both using the median family income as the point of reference.

The magnitude of poverty

As has been stressed above, the magnitude of poverty varies according to the definition of poverty adopted. Furthermore, for post-transfer poverty the estimated magnitude differs widely depending on whether public transfers counted as income include or exclude in-kind transfers. The differences resulting therefrom are illustrated by a recent study by the Congressional Budget Office.[3] According to its estimates based on the official poverty

---

[1] Robert D. Plotnick and Felicity Skidmore: Progress Against Poverty: A Review of the 1964-1974 Decade, op. cit., pp. 42-43.

[2] David M. Gordon: "Taxation of the Poor and the Normative Theory of Taxation", in American Economic Review (Menasha (Wisconsin)), Vol. LXII, No. 2, May 1972, pp. 326-327. Though not explicitly stated, the Gini coefficient seems to have been computed from the pre-tax and post-transfer money income data collected in the Current Population Survey.

[3] Congress of the United States, Congressional Budget Office: Poverty Status of Families Under Alternative Definitions of Income (Congressional Budget Office, Background Paper No. 17 (Revised), Washington, D.C., June 1977).

definition, in fiscal year 1976 when public cash transfers are counted, 10.7 million families (including unrelated individuals in the same household as one-person families) or 13.5 per cent of all families were below the official poverty line. If in-kind transfers group I (food stamps, children, nutrition and housing assistance) are added, the number of families in poverty would be reduced by 1.7 million to 9 million and the poverty incidence by 2.2 per cent to 11.3 per cent. If in-kind transfers group II (medicare and medicaid benefits) are also counted as income, the number of families in poverty would be further reduced by 2.5 million to 6.4 million and the poverty incidence by another 3.2 per cent to 8.1 per cent.[1] The Congressional Budget Office study has pointed out some of the conceptual issues raised by the inclusion of in-kind transfers and in particular the benefit-received approach to the treatment of medicare and medicaid used in the study.[2]

The review of poverty in the United States that follows is based on the concept of money income available for alternative uses with the reservation that the data used refer to money income before taxes. Thus public transfers for this review include cash transfers but not in-kind transfers. The effects of the latter in reducing poverty will be considered, however, in the next chapter.

In 1975, according to the poverty statistics of the Census Bureau which uses a pre-tax and post-transfer concept of money income, after public cash transfers about 25.9 million persons or 12.3 per cent of the population in the United States lived below the "minimum subsistence standard" prescribed by the official poverty line. Slightly above this level were 11.3 million persons or 5.3 per cent of the population living between 100 and 125 per cent of the official poverty line.[3]

It would be instructive to gain a perspective of the number of persons living at income levels successively higher than the official poverty line and the distribution of the whole population, and, conversely, the distribution of the nation's total personal income, classified on this basis. For post-transfer income the latest data were those for 1974, and they have been used for these calculations.

---

[1] Congress of the United States, Congressional Budget Office: Poverty Status of Families Under Alternative Definitions of Income (Congressional Budget Office, Background Paper No. 17 (Revised) Washington, D.C., June 1977), p. 8 and p. 22.

[2] ibid., p. 6 and p. 19. The study has stated: "In extreme cases, the benefit-received approach could count thousands of dollars in benefits as income available for alternative use. Since the current poverty levels are based on normal health expenditures which may be small for the poor, this approach implies that a family can be made non-poor by virtue of large health costs. The criticism is that this is not a fair measure of income unless the poverty levels are also adjusted to reflect a higher level of health care need."

[3] US Department of Commerce, Bureau of the Census, Current Population Reports, Consumer Income, Series P-60, No. 103: Money Income and Poverty Status of Families and Persons in the United States: 1975 and 1974 Revisions (Advance Report) (Washington, D.C., Sep. 1976), p. 34 and p. 36.

Post-transfer absolute poverty by alternative standards

Table 5 presents the number and percentage of persons classified according to the ratio of family money income after public cash transfers to the official poverty line in 1974. This classification provides a basis for making rough estimates of the number and proportion of persons that would be counted as the post-transfer poor if some alternative standards of absolute poverty were applied.

Higher poverty standards can be set by increasing the ratio of family income to the official poverty line. With the official poverty standard, 23.4 million persons fall below it. Raising the ratio by another 25 per cent would roughly add another 10 million or another 5 per cent. Thus by using 125 per cent of the official poverty line as the poverty standard, the magnitude of post-transfer poverty (after public cash transfers) would be increased from 23.4 million to 33.7 million persons and the incidence of poverty from 11 per cent to 16 per cent. If the poverty standard is set at 150 per cent of the official poverty line, the magnitude would be increased to 44 million persons and the poverty incidence to 21 per cent or almost double the official estimate for 1974.

Similarly, from table 5, crude estimates can be computed of the magnitude of poverty after public cash transfers measured by the OECD poverty standard and by BLS urban lower budgets. The estimates obtained are shown in table 6. These can only be taken as a first approximation, but what is striking is the wide disparity between these estimates and the estimate measured by the official poverty line. By the OECD standard the magnitude of poverty in 1974 would be 59 per cent greater than was found by the official poverty line: the number of persons in poverty would be 37 million or an increase of 14 million and the poverty incidence would be 17.8 per cent or an increase of 6.6 percentage points.[1] Using the BLS urban lower budget as a poverty standard yields a still higher estimate. By that measure as many as 60 million people would be in post-transfer poverty or two-and-a-half times the magnitude based on the official poverty line. Even if the BLS non-metropolitan urban lower budget was used as a measure, some 54 million persons or about one-quarter of the population would be counted as poor.

The above simple exercises in numbers tend to lend further support to the view that the official poverty line that has been in use is too low. The question at once arises: which of the higher absolute poverty standards discussed above can be considered appropriate to the present United States setting, bearing in mind that the higher the poverty standard chosen the more far-reaching are the anti-poverty measures that are needed. The question clearly involves a whole complex of political and economic issues which would be difficult to disentangle within the space of this study.

---

[1] In a study for an anti-poverty agency of the United States Catholic Conference, it was estimated that the number of poor people in 1974 was about 40 million. (The study was written by Mariellen Procopio and Frederick Parella, as reported in the International Herald Tribune, Paris, 26 Dec. 1975, p. 3.) From this estimated number it can be inferred that the poverty standard used by this study was slightly higher than the OECD standard.

Table 5

Number of Persons Classified According to the Ratio of Family Income(1) to the Official Poverty line Income in 1974

(Number in thousands of persons as of March 1975)

Ratio of family income to the official poverty line income	Number	Cumulative number	As per cent of total population	
			per cent	cumulative percentage
under 0.75	13 823	13 823	6.6	6.6
0.75 to 0.99	9 547	23 370	4.6	11.2
1.00 to 1.24	10 294	33 664	4.9	16.1
1.25 to 1.49	10 498	44 162	5.0	21.1
1.50 to 1.99	24 061	68 223	11.5	32.6
2.00 or more	141 139	209 362	67.4	100.0
All income levels	209 362			

Source: US Department, Bureau of Census, Current Population Report, Consumer Income: Series P-60, No. 103: Money Income and Poverty Status of Families and Persons in the United States: 1975 and 1974 Revisions (Advance Report) (Washington, Sep. 1976), p. 8.

(1) For unrelated individuals, income of the individual.

Table 6

Estimates of Number of Persons in Poverty in 1974 by the OECD Standard and by the BLS Urban Lower Budgets

	Poverty standard		Estimates of Number of Persons in poverty in 1974		
	in 1974 dollars	as per cent of official poverty line	in million persons	as per cent of number under official poverty line	as per cent of total population
OECD standard	6 731	133.6	37.3	159	17.8
BLS Urban lower cost budget	9 198	182.6	59.8	256	28.6
BLS Non-Metropolitan urban lower cost budget	8 639	171.5	54.5	237	26.0
Official poverty line	5 038	100.0	23.4	100	11.2

Source: Estimates computed by the writer from data given in table 5 and in other sources cited in the preceding parts of this chapter. In making these estimates of the total number of persons in poverty, the poverty standards used are all for a 4-person family on the assumption that the ratios of other poverty standards for families of other sizes do not differ significantly from their ratios to the official poverty line on a 4-person family basis.

Trends in poverty

The discussions of poverty thus far have been confined to post-transfer poverty. For the purpose of this study, however, it will be of particular interest to ascertain, where possible, the trends in poverty before and after public transfers in absolute as well as relative terms. A comparison of the pre-transfer and post-transfer trends could uncover the extent to which poverty has been reduced by the working of the socio-economic system itself, and the extent to which poverty that would have remained has been alleviated by the State through its public transfer programmes.

In the United States despite the abundant literature on poverty, the relationship of pre-transfer and post-transfer trends, absolute and relative, has been brought to light only since the recent publication of the work by Plotnick and Skidmore referred to earlier. For post-transfer income they used the same pre-tax money income concept as used in the poverty statistics of the Census Bureau. For pre-transfer income the concept used is pre-tax money income before public cash transfers (i.e. the sum of wages, salaries, property income and private transfers). Absolute poverty, both pre-transfer and post-transfer, was measured by the official poverty lines, whereas relative poverty, both pre-transfer and post-transfer, was measured by 0.44 of the median welfare ratio (welfare ratio equals income divided by the official poverty line).[1] As already indicated, this four-fold classification is of considerable use. Unfortunately, the findings of Plotnick and Skidmore are limited to four years (1965, 1968, 1970 and 1972) spanning the seven-year period from 1965 to 1972.

In what follows the main features of the trends in post-transfer poverty, the impact of public cash transfers on poverty reduction and the trends in pre-transfer poverty are briefly reviewed on the basis of the poverty statistics published by the Bureau of the Census and the findings of Plotnick and Skidmore.

(a) Trends in post-transfer poverty

For post-transfer absolute poverty measured by the official poverty lines a continuous yearly time series prepared by the Bureau of the Census is available from 1959 onwards. As it uses a money income concept, it does not include public in-kind transfers. This time series up to 1975 is reproduced in table 7 and Chart 1. Periodic revisions of the methodology used, however, have rendered difficult comparisons over different periods of time, particularly before and after 1966, and before and after 1974.

Bearing this reservation in mind, as can be seen from table 7, the size of post-transfer absolute poverty by the official definition has diminished markedly between 1959 and 1975: the number of persons below the official poverty line decreased from 39.5 to 25.9 million and the incidence of poverty from 22 per cent to 12 per cent. Over the entire period the trend can be divided into three phases: the downward phase from 1962 to 1968, the stationary phase from 1969 to 1973 and the upward phase during 1974-75.

---

[1] The reason for adopting this measure of relative poverty was explained earlier in this chapter.

Table 7 (a)

Estimated Number of Persons below the Official Poverty Line and below 125 per cent of the Official Poverty Line

1959-1975

(1) Number of Persons (in millions)

	Below official poverty line						Between 100 and 125 per cent of official poverty line						Below 125 per cent of official poverty line					
	Total		White		Black and other races		Total		White		Black and other races		Total		White		Black and other races	
	No.	Index	No.	Index	No.	Index	No.	Index	No.	Index	No.	Index	No.	Index	No.	Index	No.	Index
1959	39.5	100.0	28.5	100.0	11.0	100.0	15.4	100.0	13.3	100.0	2.1	100.0	54.9	100.0	41.8	100.0	13.1	100.0
1960	39.8	100.8	28.3	99.3	11.5	104.5	14.7	95.5	12.8	96.2	1.9	90.5	54.5	99.3	41.1	98.3	13.4	102.3
1961	39.6	100.3	27.9	97.9	11.7	106.4	14.7	95.5	12.6	94.7	2.1	100.0	54.3	98.9	40.5	96.9	13.8	105.3
1962	38.6	97.7	26.7	93.7	12.0	109.1	14.5	94.2	12.2	91.7	2.3	109.5	53.1	96.7	38.8	92.8	14.3	109.2
1963	36.4	92.2	25.2	88.4	11.2	101.8	14.4	93.5	12.0	90.2	2.4	114.3	50.8	92.5	37.2	89.0	13.6	103.8
1964	36.1	91.4	25.0	87.7	11.1	100.9	13.7	89.0	11.5	86.5	2.2	104.8	49.8	90.7	36.5	87.3	13.3	101.5
1965	33.2	84.0	22.5	78.9	10.7	97.3	13.0	84.4	10.6	79.7	2.4	114.3	46.2	84.2	33.1	79.2	13.1	100.0
1966	30.4	77.0	20.7	72.6	9.7	88.2	10.2	66.2	8.2	61.7	2.0	95.2	40.6	74.0	28.9	69.1	11.7	89.3
1966[1]	28.5	72.2	19.3	67.7	9.2	83.6	12.8	83.1	10.2	76.7	2.6	123.8	41.3	75.2	29.5	70.6	11.8	90.1
1967	27.8	70.4	19.0	66.7	8.8	80.0	11.4	74.0	9.0	67.7	2.4	114.3	39.2	71.4	28.0	67.0	11.2	85.5
1968	25.4	64.3	17.4	61.1	8.0	72.7	10.5	68.2	8.1	60.9	2.4	114.3	35.9	65.4	25.5	61.0	10.4	79.4
1969[2]	24.1	61.0	16.6	58.2	7.5	68.2	10.5	68.2	7.9	59.4	2.6	123.8	34.7	63.2	24.5	58.6	10.1	77.1
1970	25.4	64.3	17.5	61.4	7.9	71.8	10.2	66.2	7.9	59.4	2.3	109.5	35.6	64.8	25.4	60.8	10.2	77.9
1971	25.6	64.8	17.8	62.5	7.8	70.9	10.9	70.8	8.4	63.2	2.5	119.0	36.5	66.5	26.2	62.7	10.3	78.6
1972	24.5	62.0	16.2	56.8	8.3	75.5	10.2	66.2	8.0	60.1	2.2	104.8	34.7	63.2	24.2	57.9	10.5	80.2
1973	23.0	58.2	15.1	53.0	7.8	70.9	9.8	63.6	7.5	56.4	2.4	114.3	32.8	59.7	22.6	54.1	10.2	77.9
1974	24.3	61.6	16.3	57.2	8.0	72.7	10.3	66.9	7.7	57.9	2.6	123.8	34.6	63.0	24.0	57.4	10.6	80.9
1974[3]	23.4	59.2	15.7	55.1	7.6	69.1	10.3	66.9	7.8	58.6	2.6	123.8	33.7	61.4	23.5	56.2	10.2	77.9
1975	25.9	65.6	17.8	62.5	8.1	73.6	11.3	73.4	8.8	66.2	2.5	119.0	37.2	67.8	26.6	63.6	10.6	80.9

.. / ..

Table 7 (b)

Estimated Number of Persons below the Official Poverty Line and below 125 per cent of the Official Poverty Line, 1959-1975

(2) Incidence and Distribution (in percentage)

	Below official poverty line						Between 100 and 125 per cent of official poverty line						Below 125 per cent of official poverty line					
	Total		White		Negro and other races		Total		White		Negro and other races		Total		White		Negro and other races	
	Inc.*	Dis.**	Inc.	Dis.	Inc.	Dis.	Inc.	Dis.	Inc.	Dis.	Inc.	Dis.	Inc.	Dis.	Inc.	Dis.	Inc.	Dis.
1959	22.4	100	18.1	72.1	56.2	27.9	8.7	100	8.6	86.4	10.6	15.4	31.1	100	26.7	76.1	66.8	23.9
1960	22.2	100	17.8	71.0	55.9	29.0	8.2	100	8.1	87.1	9.2	12.9	30.4	100	25.9	75.4	65.1	24.6
1961	21.9	100	17.4	70.4	56.1	29.6	8.1	100	7.9	86.1	7.9	13.9	30.0	100	25.3	74.6	65.8	25.4
1962	21.0	100	16.4	69.1	55.8	30.9	7.8	100	7.5	84.0	10.8	16.0	28.8	100	23.9	73.1	66.6	26.9
1963	19.5	100	15.3	69.3	51.0	30.7	7.6	100	7.2	83.1	11.1	16.9	27.1	100	22.5	73.2	62.1	26.8
1964	19.0	100	14.9	69.2	49.6	30.8	7.3	100	6.9	83.8	9.9	16.2	26.3	100	21.8	73.3	59.5	26.7
1965	17.3	100	13.3	67.8	47.1	32.2	6.8	100	6.3	81.6	10.5	18.4	24.1	100	19.6	71.6	57.6	28.4
1966	15.7	100	12.2	68.2	41.7	31.8	5.3	100	4.8	80.0	8.9	20.0	21.0	100	17.0	71.2	50.6	28.8
1966[1]	14.7	100	11.3	67.8	39.8	32.3	6.6	100	6.0	79.9	11.1	20.1	21.3	100	17.3	71.4	50.9	28.6
1967	14.2	100	11.0	68.4	37.2	31.6	5.8	100	5.3	78.9	10.2	21.1	20.0	100	16.3	71.4	47.4	28.6
1968	12.8	100	10.0	68.5	33.5	31.5	5.4	100	4.7	77.2	10.0	22.8	18.2	100	14.7	71.0	43.5	29.0
1969[2]	12.1	100	9.5	69.0	31.0	31.0	5.3	100	4.5	74.8	11.0	25.2	17.4	100	14.0	70.7	42.0	29.3
1970	12.6	100	9.9	68.8	32.0	31.2	5.0	100	4.4	77.3	9.3	22.7	17.6	100	14.3	71.3	41.3	28.7
1971	12.5	100	9.9	69.6	30.9	30.4	5.3	100	4.7	77.1	10.0	22.9	17.8	100	14.6	71.8	40.9	28.2
1972	11.9	100	9.0	66.2	31.9	31.9	4.9	100	4.4	78.1	8.6	21.9	16.8	100	13.4	69.7	40.5	30.3
1973	11.1	100	8.4	65.9	29.6	34.1	4.7	100	4.1	76.1	8.9	23.9	15.8	100	12.5	68.9	38.5	31.1
1974	11.6	100	8.9	67.1	29.5	32.9	4.9	100	4.2	74.8	9.6	25.2	16.5	100	13.2	69.4	39.1	30.6
1974[3]	11.2	100	8.6	67.3	28.3	32.7	4.9	100	4.3	75.7	9.7	25.2	16.1	100	12.9	69.7	38.0	30.3
1975	12.3	100	9.7	68.7	29.3	31.3	5.3	100	4.8	77.9	9.0	22.1	17.6	100	14.5	71.5	38.5	28.5

Source: US Department of Commerce, Bureau of the Census: Current Population Reports: Series P-60, No. 98: Characteristics of the Low-income Population: 1973 (Washington, D.C., Jan. 1975), pp. 13-18, and Series P-60, No. 103: Money Income and Poverty Status of Families and Persons in the United States: 1975 and 1974 Revisions (Advance Report) (Washington, D.C., Sep. 1976), p. 33 and p. 36.

* = Incidence, ** = Distribution

1 Beginning of a new series based on revised methodology; 2 Beginning with the March 1970 Current Population survey data based on 1970 census population controls; 3 Beginning of a new series based on revised methodology.

CHART I

Number of Persons in Poverty (number in millions)

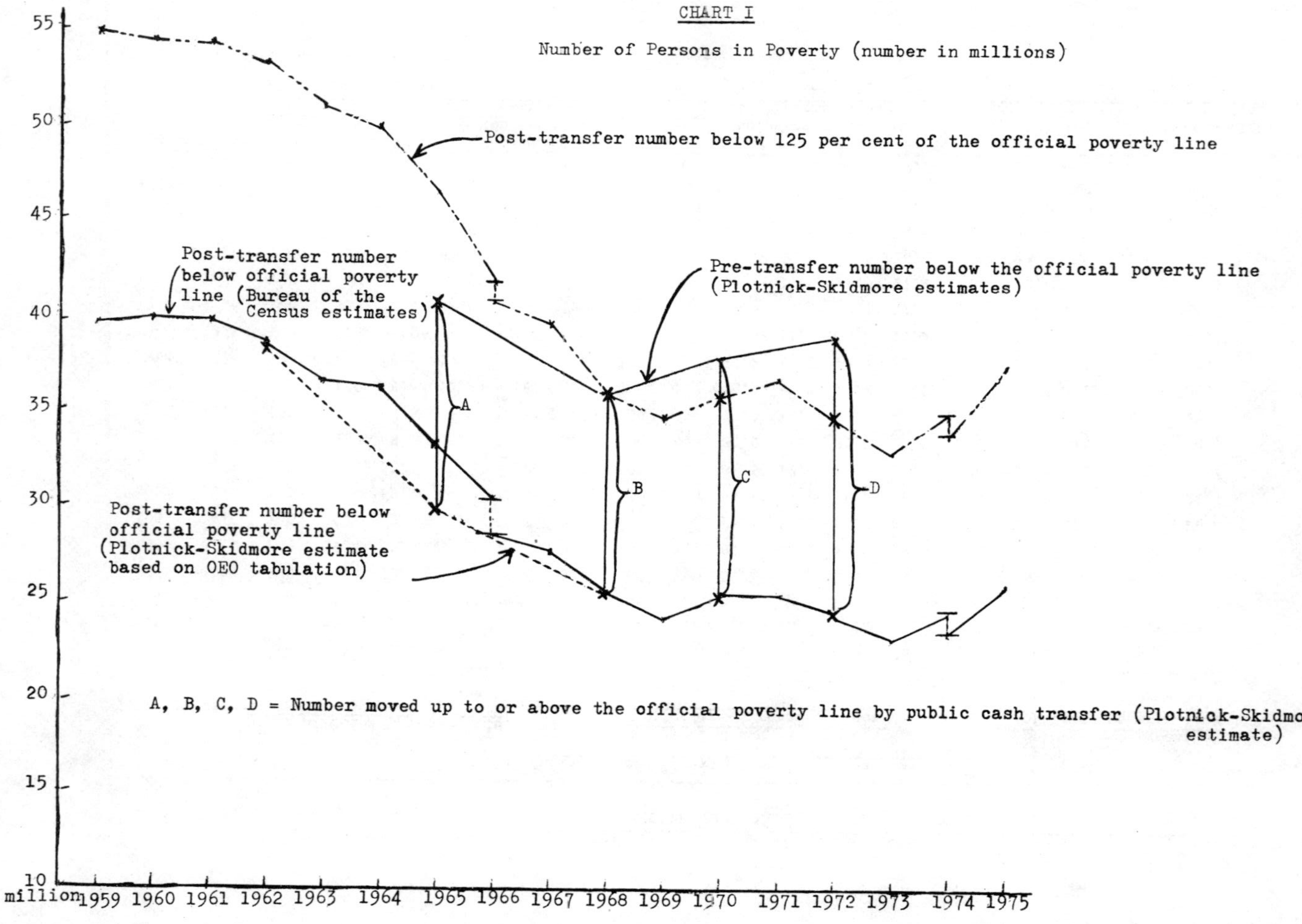
Post-transfer number below 125 per cent of the official poverty line
Post-transfer number below official poverty line (Bureau of the Census estimates)
Pre-transfer number below the official poverty line (Plotnick-Skidmore estimates)
Post-transfer number below official poverty line (Plotnick-Skidmore estimate based on OEO tabulation)
A
B
C
D
A, B, C, D = Number moved up to or above the official poverty line by public cash transfer (Plotnick-Skidmore estimate)
55
50
45
40
35
30
25
20
15
10 million
1959 1960 1961 1962 1963 1964 1965 1966 1967 1968 1969 1970 1971 1972 1973 1974 1975

The downward phase can be attributed mainly to the improved employment situation resulting from rapid economic expansion during the period associated largely with increased budget deficit to finance military expenditures for the Viet Nam war.[1] Following this was the stationary phase with the slackening of economic growth and a minor recession in 1970. Shortly after came the inflationary period which led to a severe recession and high unemployment. This brought about the upward phase of the post-transfer absolute poverty trend during 1974-75.

With regard to post-transfer relative poverty, according to the Plotnick-Skidmore estimate during the period 1965-72 the number of persons in post-transfer relative poverty by their measure actually increased from 29.9 million to 32.3 million, while the poverty incidence remained virtually constant at 15.6 and 15.7 per cent as shown in table 8. The latter, although at a lower level due to the use of a different measure, tallies with the constancy of relative poverty in a long-term perspective measured by the Fuchs point previously mentioned.

(b) The impact of public cash transfers

The movements of the post-transfer poverty trend were explained above in terms of economic changes. No reference was made to the impact of public transfers. The impact of public transfers on reducing poverty can be gauged by the difference between pre-transfer poverty and post-transfer poverty. Few estimates are available on the changes in their impact over time. The following discussion is based on the Plotnick-Skidmore estimates of pre-transfer and post-transfer poverty for the period 1965-72,[2] presented in table 8. In their estimates public transfers only cover case transfers.

Public cash transfers did increase rapidly during the period under their review. According to their lower estimates, the total amount of public cash transfers received by the pre-transfer poor (in 1972 dollars) rose from 22.4 billion in 1965 to 34.3 billion in 1972; the amount received per pre-transfer poor person increased from $549 to $870.

---

[1] For a study of the effects of employment on poverty in the United States, see R. Ferguson: "Employment and War on Poverty in the United States", in International Labour Review, Mar. 1970, pp. 247-269. See also Robert J. Lampman: Ends and Means of Reducing Income Poverty (Institute for Research on Poverty Monograph Series, University of Wisconsin, Markham Publishing Company, Chicago, 1971), pp. 80-89 and pp. 154-155.

[2] It should be noted that the post-transfer figures for absolute poverty used by Plotnick and Skidmore for their base year 1965 were lower than the corresponding figures in the Census Bureau series. For that particular year the Plotnick-Skidmore estimates were based on data from the Survey of Economic Opportunity, a special survey conducted for the Office of Economic Opportunity. For the other three years (1968, 1970 and 1972) they used the figures given in the Census Bureau's time series.

As a result of increased cash transfers, the post-transfer absolute poverty was kept at a substantially lower level than the pre-transfer poverty. Furthermore, the difference between the two levels was steadily increasing. The estimated number of pre-transfer persons in absolute poverty lifted over the official poverty line by public cash transfers rose from 10.9 million in 1965 to 12.3 million in 1972. As a percentage of the total number of persons in pre-transfer absolute poverty the number thus moved up and increased correspondingly from 27 per cent to 33 per cent, and 38 per cent.

According to their estimate, the number of persons that remained below the official poverty line after public cash transfers - the size of post-transfer absolute poverty decreased from 29.9 million in 1965 to 25.5 million in 1970 and 24.5 million in 1972. The incidence of post-transfer absolute poverty fell from 15.6 per cent to 12.6 per cent and 11.9 per cent.

It is, however, also significant that despite the increases in public cash transfers per pre-transfer poor person in real terms, the income gap (i.e. the dollar amount required to bring the post-transfer poor up to the official poverty line) per person in post-transfer absolute poverty in 1972 dollars, instead of narrowing, had widened appreciably - from $461 in 1965 to $510 in 1972. "Thus, in real terms, though the incidence of absolute poverty has been reduce, the average degree of poverty has been slowly increasing for those suffering from it."[1]

(c) <u>Trends in pre-transfer poverty</u>

Among the findings on pre-transfer poverty the following are particularly significant.

First, the level of pre-transfer absolute poverty was high even by the official standard. As the Congressional Budget Office has shown, in fiscal year 1976 without any public transfer payments about 21.4 million families (including unrelated individuals as one-person families) had incomes (before taxes) below the official poverty line. The over-all incidence of pre-transfer poverty was 27 per cent of all families or roughly one out of four families. Approximately 15.8 million of pre-transfer poor families, or 20 per cent of all families, had incomes less than 50 per cent of the poverty line. The poorest 20 per cent of families (under the upper limit of $1,812) received as little as 0.3 per cent of the total pre-transfer family income (before taxes) of the country.[2]

The Plotnick-Skidmore study revealed a similarly high level of pre-transfer absolute poverty. In 1972, according to their estimates obtained by a different estimating procedure, 17.6 million families (including unrelated individuals as a one-person family) or 24.8 per cent of all families lived in pre-transfer poverty by the official

---

[1] Robert D. Plotnick and Felicity Skidmore, op. cit., pp. 86-87.

[2] Congress of the United States, Congressional Budget Office: <u>Poverty Status of Families Under Alternative Definitions of Income</u>, op. cit., p. 8, p. 24 and p. 25.

Table 8

Pre-transfer and Post-transfer Poverty: 1965, 1968, 1970 and 1972

	Poor Persons				Poor Families				Poor Unrelated Individuals			
	Number (in thousands)		Incidence (in percentage)		Number (in thousands)		Incidence (in percentage)		Number (in thousands)		Incidence (in percentage)	
	Pre-transfer	Post-transfer	Pre-transfer	Post-transfer	Pre-transfer	Post-transfer	Pre-transfer	Post-transfer	Pre-transfer	Post-transfer	Pre-transfer	Post-transfer
Absolute Poverty												
1965	40 790	29 900	21.3	15.6	9 445	5 989	19.5	12.4	6 164	4 460	50.7	36.7
1968	35 770	25 055	18.2	12.8	8 403	5 051	16.6	10.0	6 530	4 699	47.3	34.0
1970	37 840	25 516	18.8	12.6	8 973	5 221	17.3	10.1	7 258	5 044	47.2	32.8
1972	39 440	24 494	19.2	11.9	9 607	5 075	17.7	9.3	8 033	4 896	47.9	29.2
Relative Poverty												
1965	40 790	29 900	21.3	15.6	9 445	5 989	19.5	12.4	6 164	4 460	50.7	36.7
1968	38 650	28 657	19.7	14.6	9 024	5 846	17.9	11.6	6 714	5 067	48.7	36.7
1970	41 970	30 443	20.8	15.1	9 860	6 286	19.0	12.1	7 611	5 759	49.5	37.5
1972	45 600	32 289	22.2	15.7	11 020	6 802	20.3	12.5	8 537	6 096	50.9	36.3

	Total Income Gap (in million 1972$)		Average Income Gap per poor person (in 1972$)		Cash Transfers received by Pre-transfer poor (in million 1972$)	Cash Transfers received per pre-transfer poor person (in 1972$)
Absolute Poverty						
1965	29 349	13 794	720	461	22 400	549
1968	28 590	12 241	799	489	23 400	654
1970	31 237	12 375	825	485	27 600	729
1972	34 294	12 484	870	510	34 300	870
Relative Poverty						
1965	29 349	13 749	718	461	22 400	549
1968	32 300	14 900	836	520	24 200	626
1970	37 400	16 600	891	545	28 900	689
1972	44 700	19 300	980	598	36 500	800

Source: Robert D. Plotnick and Felicity Skidmore; Progress Against Poverty: A Review of the 1964-74 Decade, op.cit., p. 82, p. 112, p. 137, p. 140. Figures for average income gap per poor person and cash transfers received per pre-transfer poor person (in 1972 $) were computed by the present writer.

standard. It covered 39.4 million or 19.2 per cent of the population. The pre-transfer income per poor family in 1972 was only $928 - compared to an average pre-transfer income of $11,596 for all multi-person families and of $4,191 for all one-person families (i.e. unrelated individuals). Moreover, between 1965 and 1972 the average pre-transfer real income per poor family had fallen and the average income gap per poor family in real terms had widened.[1]

Second, the number of persons in pre-transfer absolute poverty showed little decline between 1965 and 1972. It decreased from 40.8 million in 1965 to 35.8 million but moved steadily upwards again to 37.8 million in 1970 and 39.4 million in 1972. Similarly, the incidence, having fallen from 21.3 per cent in 1965 to 18.2 per cent in 1968, rose to 18.8 per cent in 1970 and 19.2 per cent in 1972.

Third, unlike the level of pre-transfer absolute poverty, the level of pre-transfer relative poverty kept rising year by year. Between 1965 and 1972 the number of persons in pre-transfer relative poverty increased from 40.8 million to 45.6 million, and the incidence also rose by one percentage point from 21.3 to 22.2 per cent.

An analysis of the Plotnick-Skidmore data has led to two broad conclusions on the over-all impact of public cash transfer on the magnitude of post-transfer absolute and relative poverty over the period 1965-72:

1. For absolute poverty measured by the official poverty line the public cash transfers had brought about a slow decline in incidence and had kept the number of post-transfer persons in absolute poverty fairly stable but at a rather high level.

2. For relative poverty by the Plotnick-Skidmore definition the public cash transfers had kept its incidence virtually constant but had failed in preventing the number of post-transfer persons in relative poverty from steadily rising.

(d) <u>An explanation of post-transfer poverty trends</u>

The trend of post-transfer poverty resulted from the combined movement of the pre-transfer trend and the trend of poverty reduction brought about by public transfers. The three trends have been discussed separately above. It will be useful to ascertain the relative role played by the latter two trends in shaping the post-transfer trend. Admittedly, the growth of public transfers was not independent of the pre-transfer trend. Still, there is much to be said for treating each as a separate determinant of the post-transfer poverty trend.

The change in the number of persons in post-transfer poverty A over a given period of time is the difference between the change in the number of persons in pre-transfer poverty B and the change in the number of persons lifted out of poverty by public transfers T. Symbolically:

$$A = B - T$$

---

[1] Robert D. Plotnick and Felicity Skidmore, op. cit., p. 51, pp. 86-87 and p. 118.

This simple equation can be developed into an equation describing the functional relationship between A on the one hand and B and T on the other.[1] For the present limited purpose it will suffice to use the equation as it stands.

Table 8(a) indicates the quantitative relation of A, B and T relating to four years spanning the seven-year period 1965-72 on the estimates made by Plotnick and Skidmore. The Plotnick and Skidmore estimates were, in fact, the only time series data available on pre-transfer poverty. For their estimates poverty was measured by the official poverty line and public transfers include cash transfers only.

As can be seen, during the seven-year period under review, two important changes took place. First, the trend of pre-transfer poverty declined during 1965-68 but turned upward during the subsequent four years from 1968 to 1972. Second, the trend of poverty reduction due to public transfers or the transfer effect moved in the opposite direction. The transfer effect was slightly negative between 1965 and 1968 but was increasing at an accelerating tempo between 1968 and 1972.

The movements of the post-transfer poverty trend over the period can be readily explained by the joint effect of the opposite movements of these two underlying trends:

Between 1965 and 1968: The fall in post-transfer poverty resulted from the fall in pre-transfer poverty but to a lesser extent because of a slight decrease in the transfer effect.

Between 1968 and 1970: The small increase in post-transfer poverty can be traced to an increase in pre-transfer poverty 4.5 times as large, nearly four-fifths of which was, however, offset by an increase in transfer effects. It may be noted that over this second subperiod the increased transfer effect was still weaker than the opposite effect of increased pre-transfer poverty.

Between 1970 and 1972: During this third subperiod the relative importance of the two underlying trends was reversed. A substantial decrease in post-transfer poverty occurred in the face of an even greater increase in pre-transfer poverty. This became possible only because the transfer effect had grown to such an extent that it exceeded the increased pre-transfer poverty by as much as 64 per cent.

Due to the lack of available data similar analysis was not possible for the period from 1960 to 1965 and from 1972 to 1976. Nevertheless, general observations on the changes in the economic situation and the changes in the size of public transfers tend to suggest the following patterns of relationship between the three trends in these two respective periods.

---

[1] For instance, the equation can be expanded by making B as a function of certain key variables (e.g. economic growth and unemployment) and T as a function of certain other variables (e.g. variables determining the size and effectiveness of public transfers) and by introducing interdependence between B and T.

Table 8(a)

The Relative Effects of Pre-transfer Poverty and Public Transfers on Post-transfer Poverty, 1965-1972

(Number of persons in thousands)

	Number of persons below the official poverty line				Number of persons lifted above the poverty line by public transfers		$\frac{T}{B}$
	Post-transfer		Pre-transfer				
	Number	Change over the period A	Number	Change over the period B	Number	Change over the period T	
1965	29 900		40 790		10 890		
1968	25 055	- 4 845	35 770	- 5 020	10 715	- 175	0.35
1970	25 516	461	37 840	2 070	12 324	1 609	0.78
1972	24 494	- 1 022	39 440	1 600	14 946	2 622	1.64
1965-72		- 5 406		- 1 350		4 056	3.00

Source: Figures for A, B and T were computed from the estimates of persons in pre-transfer and post-transfer absolute poverty reproduced in table 8.

The period 1960-65 saw a decline in the trend of pre-transfer poverty continuing into the second half of the 1960s as a consequence of improved employment opportunities in a process of rapid economic expansion as indicated previously. On the other hand, the amount of public transfers during that period, though on the increase, was still relatively moderate. The fall in post-transfer poverty between 1960 and 1965 was thus attributable primarily to the declining pre-transfer poverty trend with public transfers playing only a minor role.

The period 1972-76 provides a contrast. In all likelihood the rising trend of pre-transfer poverty, which began in the second half of the 1960s, was continuing into the 1974-75 recession and in later years under the conditions of high unemployment and sluggish recovery. Even though each estimate used a different estimating procedure, the fact that the estimate of the incidence of families in pre-transfer poverty for the fiscal year 1976 (27 per cent) made by the Congressional Budget Office[1] was appreciably higher than the corresponding estimate (24.8 per cent) for the calendar year 1972 made by Plotnick and Skidmore may serve as an indication of the continuation of the rising trend. However, during this recent period, public transfers were also continuing to grow rapidly, and the great expansion of expenditures on unemployment compensation deserves special notice in this connection. Unlike the period 1968-72, the continuous growth of the transfer effect was not sufficient to compensate for the increases in pre-transfer poverty. According to the Census Bureau's poverty statistics which exclude public in-kind transfers, the incidence and number of persons in post-transfer poverty increased successively in 1974 and 1975 as is shown in table 7(a) and (b).

The poverty profile

In this section on the profile of poverty the focus will be on post-transfer poverty as officially defined and shown in the Census Bureau's poverty statistics. A few words will be said first about certain long-term changes in the poverty profile that have taken place in the United States. A more detailed description will then be made of the profile of recent years illustrated by the 1975 data.

Amongst the long-term changes in the poverty profile the most significant has been the shift of relative importance from male-headed families to female-headed families and unrelated individuals[2] in the composition of the poor. As is shown in table 9, between

---

[1] Congress of the United States, Congressional Budget Office: Poverty Status of Families Under Alternative Definitions of Income, op. cit., p. 8.

[2] Figures computed from data given in US Department of Commerce, Bureau of the Census: Characteristics of the Low-income Population: 1973, op. cit., pp. 20-21 and Money Income and Poverty Status of Families and Persons in the United States: 1975 and 1974 Revisions (Advance Report), op. cit., pp. 37-41.

1959 and 1975, the share of persons living in familes with a male head in the total number of persons below the poverty line has dropped from 70 per cent to 46 per cent, while those of persons in female-headed families and of unrelated individuals have risen, respectively, from 18 to 34 per cent and from 12 to 20 per cent. This change in the composition of the poor can be attributed, to a large extent, to a much slower rate of decline in the poverty incidence of the two latter groups but also partly to an increase in their relative importance in the total population. Over these 16 years the total number of female-headed families increased by 79 per cent (from 4.2 million to 7.5 million) compared to an increase of 19 per cent in male-headed families (from 40.8 million to 48.7 million).[1] Likewise the total number of unrelated individuals increased from 10.8 million to 20.2 million or by 87 per cent compared to a 20 per cent increase in the total population.[2]

Subgroups with high poverty incidence

Subgroups with high poverty incidence are well known and are briefly discussed below.

Blacks and other minorities. The incidence of poverty among the Black population in 1975 was 31.4 per cent compared to 9.7 per cent among the White population, the incidence being over three times that for Whites. Moreover, during the period 1959-75 the number of Blacks in poverty decreased far more slowly than the corresponding number of Whites. If the poverty incidence among Blacks was the same as among Whites, the number of Blacks below the official poverty line would have been 2.3 million instead of 7.5 million, and the total number of poor population in the country in 1975 would have been 20 per cent less than it was (from about 25.9 million to 20.7 million). The corresponding poverty incidence would have been reduced by 2.5 percentage points (from 12.5 to 9.8 per cent). Apart from Blacks, there were other minorities having a high poverty incidence. The population of Spanish origin, among whom about 3 million were below the poverty line in 1975, had a poverty incidence of 26.9 per cent.[3]

Families headed by women. The exceedingly high poverty incidence among families headed by women applied to both the White and Black populations. Among Whites about 26 per cent of female-headed families were below the poverty line compared to 5.5 per cent among male-headed families. Among Blacks, one half of the female-headed families lived in poverty compared to 14.2 per cent among the male counterparts. Of a total 5.4 million families in

---

[1] Figures computed from data given in US Department of Commerce, Bureau of the Census: Characteristics of the Low-income Population: 1973, op. cit., pp. 20-21 and Money Income and Poverty Status of Families and Persons in the United States: 1975 and 1974 Revisions (Advance Report), op. cit., pp. 37-41.

[2] ibid.

[3] US Department of Commerce, Bureau of the Census: Current Population Reports: Consumer Income: Series P-60, No. 103, Money Income and Poverty Status of Families and Persons in the United States: 1975 and 1974 Revisions (Advance Report), Washington, D.C., Sep. 1976, p. 34.

Table 9

Changes in the Poverty Profile: 1959 and 1975

(Numbers in million persons. Persons as of March of the following year.)

	Persons Below the Poverty Line						Total Population			
	Number (in millions)		Composition (in percentage)		Incidence (in percentage)		Number (in millions)		Distribution (in percentage)	
	1959	1975	1959	1975	1959	1975	1959	1975	1959	1975
Persons in families with										
Male head	27.5	11.9	70	46	18.2	7.1	151.1	168.2	85.6	79.3
Female head	7.0	8.8	18	34	49.4	37.5	14.7	23.6	8.3	11.1
Unrelated individuals										
Male	1.6	1.7	4	7	36.8	19.9	4.3	8.4	2.4	4.0
Female	3.4	3.4	8	13	52.1	28.9	6.5	11.8	3.7	5.6
Total	39.5	25.9	100	100	22.4	12.3	176.6	212.0	100	100

Source: Figures for number of persons below the poverty line and for poverty incidence are from US Department of Commerce, Bureau of the Census: Current Population Reports: Consumer Income, Series P-60, No. 98: Characteristics of the Low-income Population: 1973 (Washington, D.C., Jan. 1975), pp. 13-15 and US Department of Commerce, Bureau of the Census: Current Population Reports: Consumer Income Series P-60, No. 103: Money Income and Poverty Status of Families and Persons in the United States: 1975 and 1974 Revisions (Advance Report) (Washington, D.C., Sep. 1976), pp. 34-35. Other figures including those relating to the total population were computed from the above two sets of figures.

poverty in 1975 about 45 per cent were headed by women although female-headed families still formed only 13 per cent of the total number of families (56.2 million) in the country.

Unrelated individuals. Unrelated individuals comprised only 10 per cent of the total population in 1975, yet they represented nearly 20 per cent of the poverty population. Approximately two-thirds of the 5.1 million unrelated individuals in poverty were women and one-third were men. About 42 per cent of persons in this group of the poor were 65 years and over. Roughly, four out of every five in the over 65 groups were women. The poverty incidence of the aged unrelated individuals was 31 per cent. The corresponding incidence for non-aged unrelated individuals was also high (22.1 per cent). The latter again comprised more women (58 per cent) than men (42 per cent).

The South. In the South, despite the rapid decline of poverty incidence with the progress of industrialisation, it was substantially higher among both Whites and Blacks than in the rest of the country (North and West). Among Whites the incidence in 1975 was 11.4 per cent as against 9 per cent in the North and West. Among Blacks the difference was much greater; 36.6 per cent as against 25.2 per cent, respectively. Moreover, the contrast in regional distribution of poverty population between Whites and Blacks deserves special notice. Whereas the North and East accounted for 65 per cent and the South for only 35 per cent of the White poverty population, the South accounted for 62.4 per cent, and the North and East for only 37.6 per cent of the Black poverty population.

Inside poverty areas. Certain areas in the United States are officially defined as "high poverty incidence areas"[1] and the statistics tend to bear out these demarcations. In 1975, among Whites, the incidence was 20.3 per cent inside poverty areas compared to 7.3 per cent outside these areas. Among Blacks it reached as high as over 41 per cent inside the areas compared to 20 per cent outside. Of greater interest was the difference in the degree of concentration of poverty population between Whites and Blacks. Among the White poverty population only 32 per cent lived in the poverty areas and 68 per cent were dispersed outside these areas. The reverse was true among the Black poverty population. Nearly 70 per cent of them were localised inside the poverty areas and only 30 per cent lived outside.[2] The degree of concentration has implications for anti-poverty measures. Where the poverty population is highly concentrated in particular areas measures against poverty could be more effectively taken on a local basis than where the poverty population is widely dispersed.

---

[1] For statistics on poverty status, poverty areas, in metropolitan areas are defined in terms of census tracts and in non-metropolitan areas in terms of minor civil divisions (townships, districts, etc.) in which 20 per cent or more of the population was below the poverty line in 1969. (See US Department of Commerce, Bureau of the Census: Characteristics of the Low-income Population: 1973, op. cit., p. 155.)

[2] The figures given in this paragraph were computed from data given in US Department of Commerce, Bureau of the Census: Money Income and Poverty Status of Families and Persons in the United States: 1975 and 1974 Revisions (Advance Report), op. cit., p. 43.

It is important to note that in each of the five differently classified pairs of subgroups considered above, the ones which had the lower (indeed very much lower) poverty incidence comprised a larger proportion in the whole poverty population, and its counterpart with the higher incidence represented the smaller proportion. This is due to the fact that the former, compared with the latter, had a considerably larger proportion in the total population.[1] As is shown in table 10, in 1975 Whites formed 69 per cent of the total poverty population as against 31 per cent by Blacks; male-headed families 53 per cent as against 47 per cent by female-headed families; and the North and East 57 per cent as against 43 per cent by the South. Similarly, the poverty population living outside poverty areas accounted for 57 per cent of the total compared to 43 per cent. Underlying these patterns of composition of the poor was the numerical predominance of Whites over Blacks and of male-headed families over female-headed families in the total population of the country.

Family characteristics associated with high poverty incidence

The poverty statistics of the Bureau of the Census have revealed that high poverty incidence for members of subgroups was generally associated with certain characteristics of the poor families. In this section, we discuss five such characteristics: (1) large number of children; (2) small number of earners; (3) low level of education; (4) employment status; and (5) family head in low-wage occupations. Data for 1975 are shown in tables 11 and 12. The relationship of these characteristics to poverty seems self-evident. None the less, it is worth while to examine them more closely especially in conjunction with the composition of the poor.

Large number of children. The incidence of poverty rose steadily with the number of children among those classified as poor. Among all the poor families in 1975 the incidence increased from 5 per cent in "no children" families to 30 per cent in families with five or more children. However, this relationship has lost much of its significance in the composition of the poor. The poor families with five or more children and with the highest poverty incidence formed, in fact, the smallest group (11 per cent) among all the poor families, whereas the largest single group (41 per cent)

---

[1] Symbolically, let C_a and C_b denote, respectively, the proportion of subgroup a and subgroup b in the total poverty population; I_a and I_b respectively, the poverty incidence of subgroup a and of subgroup b; and P_a and P_b respectively, the proportion of subgroup a and subgroup b in the total population. The ratio of C_a to C_b can be computed from the following equation:

$$\frac{C_a}{C_b} = \frac{(I_a)(P_a)}{(I_b)(P_b)}$$

Table 10

Selected Characteristics of Persons Below the Official Poverty Line: 1966, 1973, 1975

(Persons as of March of the following year)

Characteristics	Number of Persons (in thousands)			Incidence (in percentage)			Composition (in percentage)		
	1966	1973	1975[a]	1966	1973	1975[a]	1966	1973	1975[a]
Total number of persons below the poverty line	28 510	22 973	25 877	14.7	11.1	12.3			
Race									
White	19 290	15 142	17 770	11.3	8.4	9.7	67.7	65.9	68.7
Black and other races	9 220	7 831	8 107	39.8	29.6	29.3	32.3	34.1	31.3
Black	8 867	7 388	7 545	41.8	31.4	31.3	31.1	32.2	29.2
Family status									
In families	23 809	18 299	20 789	13.1	9.7	10.9	83.5	79.7	80.3
Unrelated individuals	4 701	4 674	5 088	38.3	25.6	25.1	16.5	20.3	19.7
White	3 860	3 730	3 972	36.1	23.7	22.7			
Black	777	828	1 011	54.4	37.9	42.1			
65 years and over			2 125			31.0			8.2
Under 65 years			2 963			22.1			11.5
In families by sex of head									
Male head	16 948	10 121	11 943	10.3	6.0	7.1	71.2	55.3	57.4
White	11 748	7 409	9 221	8.0	4.9	6.1	49.3	40.5	44.3
Black	4 930	2 496	2 365	33.0	17.7	16.9	20.7	13.6	11.4
Female head	6 861	8 178	8 846	39.8	37.5	37.5	28.8	44.7	42.6
White	3 646	4 003	4 577	29.7	28.0	29.4	15.3	21.9	22.0
Black	3 160	4 064	4 168	65.3	56.5	54.3	13.3	22.2	20.0
Age									
65 years and over	5 114	3 354	3 317	28.5	16.3	15.3	17.9	14.6	12.8
White	4 357	2 698	2 634	26.4	14.4	13.4			
Black	722	620	652	55.1	37.1	36.3			
Under 65 years	23 396	19 614	22 573	13.3	10.5	12.0	82.1	85.4	87.2
Region									
North and West	14 793[b]	12 912	14 818	10.8[b]	9.1	10.4	53.3[b]	56.2	57.3
South	12 976[b]	10 061	11 059	22.1[b]	15.3	16.2	46.7[b]	43.8	42.7
Type of Residence									
Inside Metropolitan areas	13 832[b]	13 759	15 348	10.9[b]	9.7	10.8	49.8[b]	59.9	59.3
Inside central cities	8 649[b]	8 594	9 090	15.0[b]	14.0	15.0	31.1[b]	37.4	31.5
In poverty areas		4 363	4 446		32.4	34.9		19.0	17.2
Outside central cities	5 183[b]	5 165	6 259	8.1[b]	6.4	7.6	18.7[b]	22.5	24.2
In poverty areas		1 029	900		22.9	20.8		4.5	3.5
Outside metropolitan areas	13 936[b]	9 214	10 529	20.0[b]	14.0	15.4	50.2[b]	40.1	40.7
In poverty areas		5 257	5 739		22.4	23.7		22.9	22.2

Source: US Department of Commerce, Bureau of the Census: Characteristics of the Low-Income Population 1973, op. cit., and Money Income and Poverty: Status of Families and Persons in the United States: 1975 and 1974 Revisions (Advanced Report) op. cit.

(a) New series based on revised methodology. (b) Figure refers to 1967.

had only one or two children. And poor families with no children were quantitatively (23 per cent) almost as important as those with two to four children. This phenomenon tends to suggest that children's allowance by itself would not be an effective instrument in dealing with the over-all size of poverty.

Smaller number or absence of earners. Poverty incidence varied inversely with the number of workers in the family. That poor families with no earners had the highest incidence was to be expected. More revealing, however, was a marked drop in the average poverty incidence from nearly 11 per cent for a one-worker family to 4 per cent for a two-worker family. This sudden drop was discernable among Whites and more so among Blacks. In terms of composition of poor families, one-worker families in 1975 formed nearly as high a proportion (38 per cent) of the total as families with no workers (40 per cent), while two-worker families accounted for no more than 16 per cent of the total. In absolute numbers among 5.4 million poor families in the country in 1975, about 2.1 million were one-worker families - only slightly less in number than no-worker families (2.2 million). The number of two-worker poor families was only 0.9 million. The presence of a second worker in poor families thus has been crucial in lifting themselves above the poverty line.

Low education attainment. As demonstrated by the 1975 data, the average poverty incidence fell from 12.6 per cent among family heads with only eight years of elementary education to 6.2 per cent among heads with four years of high-school education and to 2.7 per cent among heads with a college education. At the same level of education attainment, however, the incidence was much higher among Blacks than among Whites, and among females than among males. Among male-headed poor families the poverty incidence at the three different levels of education of the male head decreased successively from 9.2 to 3.4 and 2.3 per cent, whereas among female-headed poor families the corresponding incidence decreased from 28.4 to 19.7 and to 9.8 per cent. Classified further by race, within male-headed poor families the poverty incidence for those with a White family head at the three different levels of education fell from 8.7 to 3.0 to 2.2 per cent, whereas the corresponding incidence for poor families with a Black family head fell from 16.2 to 8.0 to 3.5 per cent. In regard to the composition of poor families, the largest single group (48 per cent of the total number of poor families) were those with heads with a high-school education rather than those with only an elementary education largely because the former formed a larger proportion in the total population.

Unemployment. Among all poor families in 1975 those with an unemployed family head had, on average, a poverty incidence (21 per cent) about four times as high as families whose family heads were employed (5 per cent) but slightly lower than those with family heads not in the labour force (23 per cent). The latter group, however, included a sizeable number of "discouraged workers" who were unemployed but were not actively seeking jobs because they felt that jobs were not available. As is shown in table 11, families with unemployed heads formed only about 9 per cent of the total number of poor families, while one half of the total were those with heads not in the labour force. Though relevant data were not readily available, with the inclusion of "discouraged workers", the percentage share of the unemployed in the composition of the poor should be expected to be significantly higher than the figure given in table 11.

Table 11

Selected Characteristics of Families Below the Official Poverty Line: 1975
(Families as of March 1976)

	Number of Families (in thousands)			Incidence (in percentage)			Composition (in percentage)		
	Total	White	Black	Total	White	Black	Total	White	Black
Total number of families below the poverty line	5 450	3 838	1 513	9.7	7.7	27.1			
Number of related children under 18 years									
No children	1 278	1 061	199	5.1	4.6	11.7	23.4	27.6	13.1
1 and 2 children	2 263	1 612	620	10.2	8.3	25.7	41.5	42.0	41.0
3 and 4 children	1 309	863	413	17.1	13.2	41.5	24.0	22.5	27.3
5 and more children	599	302	282	37.8	27.9	59.7	11.0	7.9	18.6
Number of workers									
No worker	2 174	1 456	688	31.1	24.6	68.9	39.9	37.9	45.5
1 worker	2 069	1 472	567	10.9	8.8	29.1	38.0	38.4	37.5
2 workers	883	673	180	4.1	3.5	9.5	16.2	17.5	11.9
3 workers	295	209	77	3.7	2.9	11.4	5.4	5.4	5.1
Family head									
Male	3 020	2 444	509	6.2	5.5	14.2	55.4	63.7	33.6
Female	2 430	1 394	1 004	32.5	25.9	50.1	44.6	36.3	66.4
Educational attainment of head									
Total: 25 years old and over	4 600	3 261	1 249	8.8	7.0	24.9			
Elementary: Total	1 922	1 365	530	17.9	15.3	31.2	41.8	41.9	42.4
8 years	629	488	133	12.6	10.9	28.5	13.7	15.0	10.6
Male	393	342	47	9.2	8.7	16.2	8.5	10.5	3.8
Female	236	146	86	33.6	28.4	48.9	5.1	4.5	6.9
High school: Total	2 208	1 495	669	8.7	6.6	26.2	48.0	45.8	53.6
4 years	1 090	787	276	6.2	4.9	19.4	23.7	24.1	22.1
male	516	421	71	3.4	3.0	8.0	11.2	12.9	5.7
Female	575	367	205	23.7	19.7	38.0	12.5	11.2	16.4

(continued on next page)

Table 11 (contd.)

	Number of Families (in thousands)			Incidence (in percentage)			Composition (in percentage)		
	Total	White	Black	Total	White	Black	Total	White	Black
College: Total	470	401	49	3.0	2.7	6.5	10.2	12.3	3.9
Male	336	301	20	2.3	2.2	3.5	7.3	9.2	1.6
Female	134	101	29	10.9	9.8	16.1	2.9	3.1	2.3
Employment status of head									
Employed	2 154	1 628	474	5.2	4.4	13.9	39.5	42.4	31.3
Male	1 526	1 256	221	14.1	3.7	8.8	28.0	32.7	14.6
Female	629	372	253	16.7	13.2	28.0	11.5	9.7	16.7
Unemployed	505	361	135	21.2	18.4	35.8	9.3	9.4	8.9
Male	289	244	41	14.7	14.3	17.4	5.3	6.4	2.7
Female	216	117	95	52.7	45.8	65.9	4.0	3.0	6.3
Not in labour force	2 761	1 821	902	23.0	18.0	52.8	50.7	47.4	59.6
Male	1 176	917	246	13.5	11.7	32.3	21.6	23.9	16.3
Female	1 585	905	656	47.8	39.1	68.6	29.1	23.6	43.4
In Armed Forces	30	28	2	3.9	4.0	2.2	0.5	0.7	0.1
Male	30	28	2	3.9	4.0	2.2	0.5	0.7	0.1

Source: US Department of Commerce, Bureau of the Census: Money Income and Poverty Status of Families and Persons in the United States: 1975 and 1974 Revisions (Advance Report), op. cit.

Table 12

Families Below the Official Poverty Line Classified According to Occupation of Longest Job of Head: 1975
(Families as of March 1976)

Occupation of Longest Job of head	Number of Families (in thousands)							Incidence (in percentage)					
		MALE			FEMALE			MALE			FEMALE		
	Grand Total	Total	White	Black	Total	White	Black	Total	White	Black	Total	White	Black
Head worked	2 745	1 857	1 533	272	887	518	362	4.6	4.1	9.5	20.3	16.1	33.0
Professional and managerial workers	303	264	232	22	39	31	8	2.1	1.9	6.7	5.4	5.2	7.8
Clerical and Sales workers	297	104	98	3	194	136	57	2.2	2.3	1.2	12.0	10.2	20.8
Craft and kindred workers	384	377	328	42	7	1	5	4.0	3.7	8.3	(a)	(a)	(a)
Operatives, including Transport workers	513	346	284	54	167	98	67	5.0	4.6	6.7	24.9	21.1	34.0
Service workers, including private household	617	174	117	44	443	228	210	6.5	5.4	9.7	36.9	32.4	43.6
Labourers, except farm	244	219	168	48	25	15	10	9.9	9.4	12.4	(a)	(a)	(a)
Farmers and farm labourers	386	373	307	57	14	9	4	21.4	19.3	46.7	(a)	(a)	(a)

../..

Source: US Department of Commerce, Bureau of the Census: Current Population Reports: Consumer Income: Series P-60, No. 103: Money Income and Poverty Status of Families and Persons in the United States: 1975 and 1974 Revisions (Advanced Report) (Washington, D.C., Sep. 1976), pp. 37-40.

(a) Base less than 75,000.

(continued on next page)

Table 12 (contd.)

Occupation of Longest Job of head	Composition (in percentage)						Number of families (in thousands)		Incidence (in percentage)			Composition (in percentage)		
	M A L E			F E M A L E										
	Total	White	Black	Total	White	Black	White	Black	Grand Total	White	Black	Grand Total	White	Black
Head worked	100	100	100	100	100	100	2 051	634	6.1	5.1	16.1	100	100	100
Professional and managerial workers	14.2	15.1	8.1	4.4	6.0	2.5	263	30	2.2	2.0	7.0	11.0	12.8	4.7
Clerical and Sales workers	5.6	6.4	1.0	21.9	26.2	15.7	235	60	4.7	4.1	11.5	10.8	11.5	9.5
Craft and kindred workers	20.3	21.4	15.4	0.8	0.2	1.4	329	48	4.1	3.7	9.2	14.0	16.0	7.6
Operatives, including Transport workers	18.6	18.5	19.9	18.8	18.9	18.5	382	121	6.7	5.8	12.1	18.7	18.6	19.1
Service workers, including private households	9.4	7.6	16.2	49.9	44.0	58.0	344	254	15.9	12.0	27.2	22.5	16.8	40.0
Labourers, except farm	11.8	11.0	17.6	2.8	2.9	2.8	182	58	10.7	10.0	14.3	8.9	8.9	9.1
Farmers and farm labourers	20.1	20.0	21.0	1.6	1.7	1.1	316	62	21.8	19.5	20.9	14.1	15.4	10.0

(Source on previous page)

Heads in low-wage occupations. In 1975 in one half (2.7 million families) of the poor families, the family head worked the entire year.[1] More specifically, 61 per cent of the male and 36 per cent of female-headed households worked full or part-time yet could not escape poverty. Among male heads in this group the poverty incidence was particularly high among "farmers and farm labourers" (21.4 per cent) and non-farm labourers (9.9 per cent). The incidence, though not so high, was above the average among service workers (6.5 per cent) and operatives (5 per cent). The male heads in these four occupational groups accounted for 60 per cent of the total number in this subgroup. The female heads who worked during the year had a considerably higher poverty incidence (20 per cent) than the male counterparts (4.1 per cent). Moreover, unlike the males, they were concentrated in three occupations - clerical and sales workers, operatives, and service workers. Among the female working heads, service workers had a poverty incidence as high as 40 per cent followed by operatives (25 per cent). These two occupations combined represented 69 per cent of the total number of poor families with female working heads. Since these occupational classifications are known to be low-wage ones, one can understand why the incidence of poverty in them is greater than the average. The wages they earned were not sufficient to bring their families above the poverty line. Furthermore, many of them worked only part-time. They were among the "working poor" to whom a growing amount of research has been directed.[2] One recent study led to the conclusion that "low earnings are at least as much a problem as unemployment".[3]

After having considered the five family characteristics separately, a few general observations may be made. First, these characteristics are often inter-related. For example, those who were more susceptible to unemployment or remained in low-wage occupations were, in the main, workers at lower levels of educational attainment and consequently with less formally acquired skills.

---

[1] See US Department of Commerce, Bureau of the Census: Money Income and Poverty Status of Families and Persons in the United States: 1975 and 1974 Revisions (Advance Report), op. cit., p. 37.

[2] Cf., for example, Charles T. Steward, Jr., Low-wage Workers in an Affluent Society (Nelson Hall, Chicago, 1974); Barry Bluestone, William M. Murphy and Mary Stevenson: Low Wages and the Working Poor (PolicyPapers in Human Resources and Industrial Relations 22, Ann Arbor, Michigan, July 1973); David M. Gordon: Theories of Poverty and Underemployment (Lexington Books, D.C. Heath and Co., Lexington, Toronto, London, 1972); T. Vietorisz, R. Mier, J. Giblin: "Sub-employment: exclusion and inadequacy indices" in US Department of Labour: Monthly Labour Review, Vol. 98, No. 5, May 1975, pp. 3-12, and Peter Henle: "Exposing the distribution of earned income", in US Department of Labour: Monthly Labour Review, Vol. 95, No. 15, Dec. 1972, pp. 16-27.

[3] Sar A. Levitan and Robert Taggart: "Employment and Earnings Inadequacy: A New Social Indicator", in Challenge (White Plains, New York), Jan./Feb. 1974, p. 26.

Furthermore, male family heads in low-wage occupations were more likely to have a second worker in the family than those in higher wage occupations. Second, when any of these characteristics were used for classifying the poor, within the same subgroup thus classified, non-Whites and females almost invariably had a higher poverty incidence than their White or male counterparts. This can be interpreted as partial evidence of race and sex discrimination. Third, a high poverty incidence of a given subgroup may or may not be associated with a high share of this subgroup in the composition of the poor, depending on the quantitative relationship of its incidence to its share in the total population. This point may have some practical implications for anti-poverty policies. Finally, as indicated earlier, the poverty data used for analysis of the profile of poverty were post-transfer data. They already embody the effects of public cash transfers. The nature and extent of these effects on the poverty profile will be considered in the next chapter.

Chapter 2

Fiscal expenditures for poverty alleviation

This chapter attempts to analyse at some length the fiscal expenditures having a direct bearing on poverty alleviation. The fiscal expenditures to be considered in this connection are primarily the public social welfare expenditures, federal as well as state and local. The first section provides an overview of these expenditures. In the second section a more detailed review is made of the major anti-poverty programmes. In the third section the impact of these expenditures on poverty reduction will be discussed in the light of the available estimates. The last section brings into sharper focus drawbacks of the major programmes covered by these expenditures from the point of view of poverty alleviation.

Public social welfare expenditure: an overview

Public social welfare expenditures in the United States are defined as "cash benefits, services and administrative costs of all programmes operating under public law that are of direct benefit to individuals and families".[1] Most, if not all, of the fiscal expenditures having a direct effect on poverty alleviation fall under this broad heading.

Size. Total public social welfare expenditures underwent a phenomenal growth in the United States over the 15-year period from 52.3 billion dollars in 1960, to 77.2 billion in 1965, 145.8 billion in 1970 and 286.5 billion in 1975. As is shown in table II.1, between 1960 and 1975 the total annual amount incurred in constant dollars increased by 230 per cent and the amount on a per capita basis in 1975 dollars rose from 475 to 1,319 dollars or by 178 per cent. Over the same period public social welfare expenditures increased from 38 per cent to 58.4 per cent as a percentage of all government expenditures (federal, state and local combined) and from 10.6 per cent to 20.1 per cent as a percentage of GNP (see table II.2). These latter figures give an indication of the growing importance of public and social welfare expenditures in the economy. Since public social welfare expenditures are not directly productive yet raise the level of consumption, a relative increase in these expenditures would bring in its train a secondary income-generating effect, an inflation-generating effect or a combination of both, depending on the relative strength of price and output responses of the economy.

---

[1] Alfred M. Skolnik and Sophie R. Dales: "Social Welfare Expenditures, 1950-1975 in US Department of Health, Education and Welfare, Social Security Administration", Social Security Bulletin, Vol. 29, No. 1, Jan. 1976, p. 3.

Table II.1 Total and Per Capita Social Welfare Expenditures under Public Programmes in the United States in constant 1975 dollars, Selected Fiscal Years, 1950-75

	Total public social welfare expenditure (in million dollars)[a]			Per capita public social welfare expenditure in constant 1975 dollars															
	in current dollars	in constant 1975 dollars		Total		Social insurance		Veterans' programmes		Public aid		Other social welfare		Education		Health and medical programmes		All health and medical care	
Year	Amount	Amount	Index	Amount	Index	Amount	Index	Amount	Index	Amount	Index	Amount	Index	Amount	Index	Amount	Index	Amount	Index
1950	23421	48895	56.4	318	66.9	67	38.3	92	187.7	34	91.9	6	60	91	56.9	28	68.3	42	72.4
1955	32512	59764	68.9	358	75.4	108	61.7	52	106.1	33	89.2	7	70	123	76.9	34	82.9	50	86.2
1960	52106	86699	100.0	475	100.0	175	100.0	49	100.0	37	100.0	10	100	160	100.0	41	100.0	58	100.0
1965	76929	120957	139.5	615	129.5	224	128.0	48	98.0	50	135.1	17	170	224	140.0	50	122	76	131.0
1970	145389	195153	225.1	941	198.1	352	201.1	58	118.4	107	289.2	27	270	329	205.6	63	153.7	163	281.0
1972	190910	238043	274.0	1125	236.8	439	250.9	67	136.7	154	416.2	32	320	351	219.4	75	182.9	196	337.9
1973	213797	257897	297.5	1209	254.5	485	277.1	73	149.0	162	437.8	33	330	370	231.2	75	182.9	206	355.2
1974	238656	264585	305.2	1232	259.4	508	290.3	72	146.9	165	445.9	37	370	362	226.2	74	180.5	211	363.8
1975[b]	285819	285819	329.7	1319	277.7	567	324.0	76	155.1	187	505.4	36	360	362	226.2	77	187.8	231	398.3

Source: Alfred M. Skolnik and Sophie R. Dales: "Social Welfare Expenditures, 1950-75" in US Department of Health, Education and Welfare, Social Security Administration: Social Security Bulletin, Vol. 39, No. 1, Jan. 1976, p. 10. The indices were computed by the writer.

a. Excludes expenditures within foreign countries for education, veterans' payments, and OASDHI and civil service retirement benefits.

b. Preliminary estimates.

Table II.2 Public Social Welfare Expenditures, Selected Fiscal Years, 1950-75 (in million current dollars)

	Federal funds		State and local funds		Total social welfare expenditure from public funds						
						Distribution (in percentage)		As per cent of			
									Gross National Product		
	Amount	As per cent of all Federal Government expenditures	Amount	As per cent of all state and local government expenditure	Amount [a]	Federal	State and local	All government expenditures	Total	Federal	State and local
1950	10 541	26.2	12 967	60.1	23 508	44.8	55.2	37.6	8.9	4.0	4.9
1955	14 623	22.3	18 017	55.3	32 640	44.8	55.2	32.7	8.6	3.9	4.7
1960	24 957	28.1	27 337	58.3	52 293	47.7	52.3	38.0	10.6	5.0	5.5
1965	37 712	32.6	39 463	61.7	77 175	48.9	51.1	42.4	11.8	5.8	6.0
1970	77 334	40.1	68 427	62.3	145 761	53.1	46.9	47.8	15.3	8.1	7.2
1972	106 312	47.4	85 101	63.6	191 414	55.5	44.5	53.1	17.4	9.7	7.7
1973	122 611	50.5	91 779	64.2	214 390	57.2	42.8	55.3	17.5	10.0	7.5
1974	137 654	52.5	101 648	61.7	239 303	57.5	42.5	55.9	17.7	10.2	7.5
1975 [b]	165 943	54.9	120 603	64.4	286 547	57.9	42.1	58.4	20.1	11.7	8.5

Source: Alfred M. Skolnik and Sophie R. Dales: "Social Welfare Expenditures: 1950-1975", in US Department of Health, Education, and Welfare, Social Security Administration: Social Security Bulletin, Vol. 39, No. 1, Jan. 1976, pp. 6-8, pp. 12-13.

a. Includes expenditures within foreign countries for education, veterans' payments, and OASDHI and civil service retirement benefits.

b. Preliminary estimates.

Federal and state/local funds. The public social welfare expenditures were incurred under a large number of specific public programmes. Many of these programmes were financed wholly from federal funds; many others were financed jointly by Federal and state and local governments; still others wholly from state and/or local funds. Classifying public social welfare expenditures by source of funds reveals two important facts. First, there was a secular rise in the proportion financed from federal funds and a corresponding decline in the proportion financed from state and local funds. While the former increased steadily from 47.7 per cent in 1960 to 57.9 per cent in 1975, the latter decreased correspondingly from 52.3 to 42.1 per cent. It may be noted that the proportion from state and local funds, though on the decline, was still high. Second, as the size of these expenditures was expanding, the proportion of total expenditure of respective levels of government allotted to social welfare expenditure was also increasing. As is shown in table II.2, in 1975 over one-half (55 per cent) of the total expenditure of the Federal Government was allotted to these expenditures compared with 28 per cent in 1960. The proportion of the total expenditure of state and local governments thus allotted, was also on the increase, though not nearly as rapidly - from 58 per cent in 1960 to 64 per cent in 1975.

That social welfare expenditures by 1975 had grown to such a size as to absorb well over one-half of the total expenditure of both the Federal and state/local governments points to the vulnerability of these expenditures to any restraining influence exerted on the size of the federal or state and local budgets. A tightening of the over-all budget, as, for instance, for control of inflation in the case of the federal budget or to avoid the danger of bankruptcy due to inability to repay accumulated short-term debts as in the case of New York City, could perhaps leave little choice but to cut down, even if only in relative terms, allocations to social welfare expenditures. This, of course, has adverse repercussions on poverty alleviation. Further, a great many of the social welfare programmes run by state and local governments depend partly on federal financing (either on a matching basis or through revenue-sharing). Thus, the size of the federal budget or its relative allocation to social welfare expenditures has a larger impact on poverty alleviation than the state and local budgets. This is true especially when one considers the nature of social welfare programmes financed from federal funds, as will be shown presently.

Income maintenance and human investment. The vast amount of public social welfare expenditure can be divided into two broad groups according to the primary purpose of different programmes: income maintenance and human investment. One rough way of doing this is to place social insurance, veterans' programmes, public aid, food assistance, medical assistance, housing and "other social welfare" programmes in the income maintenance group, and to place education and "health and medical programmes" in the human investment group. Table II.3 presents in detail the amounts spent in current dollars on these programmes from federal funds and from state and local funds in selected fiscal years over the last-quarter century (1950-75). A summary is given in table II.4.

Table II.3

Composition of Public Social Welfare Expenditures in Selected Fiscal Years: 1950, 1965 and 1975

(in billions of current dollars)

	1950			1965			1975[1]		
	Federal	State and local	Total	Federal	State and local	Total	Federal	State and local	Total
Total	10.5	13.0	23.5	37.7	39.4	77.2	165.9	120.6	286.5
Income Maintenance	9.78	4.94	14.7	32.5	10.3	42.8	148.9	42.6	191.6
(a) Cash transfers	5.3	4.10	9.4	28.9	8.2	37.1	107.0	32.1	139.2
Social Insurance	2.1	2.8	4.9	21.8	6.3	28.1	84.4	24.2	108.7
OSDHI (excl.Midicare)	0.8		0.8	17.0		17.0	63.7		63.7
Public and railroad employee retirement	0.8	0.3	1.1	3.9	1.7	5.6	15.8	7.3	23.1
Workmen's compensation	0.02	0.6	0.6	0.08	1.8	1.9	1.4	5.1	6.4
Unemployment insurance and employment service[2]	0.4	1.9	2.3	0.8	2.3	3.1	3.6	10.9	14.4
Veterans' pensions and compensation	2.1		2.1	4.1		4.1	7.6		7.6
Public aid	1.1	1.3	2.4	3.0	1.9	4.9	15.0	7.9	22.9
SSI[2]							4.6	1.4	6.0
Public Assistance	1.1	1.3	2.4	2.6	1.9	4.0	7.1	6.5	10.4
OAA, AB, APTD[3]			1.5			2.1			
AFDC[4]			0.5			1.6			9.2
General assistance			0.3			0.3			1.1
Social services							1.9	0.6	2.5
Other	0.01		0.01	0.4		0.4	3.2		3.2
(b) Non-cash (in-kind) transfers	4.48	0.84	5.31	3.58	2.1	5.60	41.9	10.5	52.4
Food	0.12	0.09	0.2	0.54	0.1	0.64	6.7	0.5	7.2
Food stamps				0.04		0.04	4.7		4.7
Child nutrition	0.12	0.04	0.16	0.5	0.1	0.6	2.0	0.5	2.5
Medical assistance		0.05	0.05	0.6	0.8	1.4	21.8	6.0	27.8
Midicare (for the aged)							14.8		14.8
Medicaid							7.0	6.0	13.0
Housing	0.01		0.01	0.24	0.08	0.32	2.4	0.6	3.0
Public housing	0.01		0.01	0.2		0.20	1.5		1.5
Other	(a)			(a)			0.9		0.9
Other social welfare	0.05	0.2	0.25	0.3	1.1	1.4	2.1	3.2	5.3
Veterans' programme	4.3	0.5	4.8	1.9	0.02	1.92	8.9	0.2	9.1
Human Investment	0.8	8.0	8.8	5.3	29.1	34.3	17.1	78.0	95.0
Education	0.2	6.5	6.7	2.5	25.6	28.1	8.7	69.8	78.4
Elementary and secondary	0.05	5.5	5.6	0.8	21.6	22.4	4.3	53.6	57.9
Higher	0.05	0.9	0.9	1.2	3.6	4.8	3.0	13.0	16.0
Vocational and adult	0.06	0.1	0.16	0.4	0.4	0.8	1.1	3.2	4.3
Health and medical programmes	0.6	1.5	2.1	2.8	3.5	6.2	8.4	8.2	16.6

Source: Unless otherwise indicated, data for this table were from Alfred M. Skolnik and Sophie R. Dales: "Social Welfare Expenditures, 1950-1975", loc. cit., pp.6-8; data on OAA, AB, APTD, AFDC and general assistance were from US Dept. of Health, Education and Welfare: Social Security Bulletin, Vol. 39, No. 11, Nov. 1976, table M-33, p. 76. (1) Preliminary estimates; (2) SSI for Supplemental Security Income; (3) OAA for Old-age assistance; AB for Aid to the Blind; APTD for aid to permanently and totally disabled; (4) AFDC for Aid to families with dependent children. (a) less than 10 million dollars.

Table II.4 Distribution of Public Expenditures on Income Maintenance Programmes and Human Investment Programmes between Federal Funds and States-local Funds in Selected Fiscal Years 1950-1975

(amount in billions of current dollars; distribution in percentage)

Year	Total public social welfare expenditure			Income Maintenance Programmes: Cash transfers			Income Maintenance Programmes: Non-cash transfers			Income Maintenance Programmes: Total income maintenance		
		Distribution			Distribution			Distribution			Distribution	
	Amount	Federal	State-local	Amount	Federal	State-local	Amount	Federal	State-local	Amount	Federal	State-local
1950	23.5	44.7%	53.7%	9.4	56.4%	43.6%	5.3	84.9%	15.1%	14.7	66.4%	33.6%
1955	32.6	44.8	55.2	15.3	69.3	30.7	3.2	78.0	22.0	18.4	71.0	29.0
1960	52.3	47.6	52.2	26.3	74.5	25.5	3.6	77.0	23.0	29.9	74.8	25.2
1965	77.2	48.8	51.0	37.1	77.9	22.1	5.7	63.0	37.0	42.8	75.9	24.1
1970	145.8	53.0	46.9	63.6	78.6	21.4	21.4	78.0	22.0	85.0	78.5	21.5
1972	191.4	55.5	44.5	88.7	77.7	22.3	30.4	80.3	19.7	119.1	78.3	21.7
1973	214.4	57.2	42.8	100.4	79.8	20.2	35.2	80.1	19.6	135.6	79.9	20.1
1974	239.3	57.5	42.5	113.2	79.9	20.1	41.3	79.4	20.6	154.5	79.8	20.2
1975	286.5	57.9	42.1	139.2	76.9	23.1	52.4	80.0	20.0	191.6	77.7	22.2

Source: Same as table II.3.

.. / ..

Table II.4 (contd.)

Year	Human Investment Programmes								
	Education			Health and medical programmes			Total human investment		
	Amount	Distribution: Federal	Distribution: State-local	Amount	Distribution: Federal	Distribution: State-local	Amount	Distribution: Federal	Distribution: State-local
1950	6.7	3%	97%	2.1	28.6	71.4%	8.8	9.1%	90.9%
1955	11.2	4.0	96.0	3.1	35.5	64.5	14.3	11.2	88.8
1960	17.6	5.0	95.0	4.5	38.6	61.4	22.1	11.8	88.2
1965	28.1	9.0	91.0	6.2	44.4	55.6	34.3	15.4	84.6
1970	50.9	11.6	88.4	9.8	49.0	51.0	60.7	17.6	82.4
1972	59.6	11.2	88.8	12.7	49.6	50.4	72.3	18.0	82.0
1973	65.4	11.3	88.7	13.2	50.8	49.2	78.6	17.9	82.1
1974	70.1	10.0	90.0	14.4	49.6	50.3	84.5	16.8	83.2
1975	78.4	11.0	89.0	16.6	50.6	49.4	95.0	18.0	82.0

According to this rough classification a larger proportion of the public social welfare expenditure was spent on income maintenance programmes than on human investment ones. Moreover, the proportion has been increasing steadily over the past 15 years. Between 1960 and 1975 the proportion absorbed by income maintenance programmes rose from 57 per cent to 67 per cent while that allotted to human investment declined correspondingly from 42 to 33 per cent. In each broad group the role played by federal funds and by state and local funds was markedly different. Federal funds financed over 70 per cent of the income maintenance programmes as a while, whereas state and local funds financed over 80 per cent of the human investment programmes. Over the period the Federal Government was gaining relative influence not only in the income maintenance sphere (from 75 per cent in 1960 to 78 per cent in 1975) but also in the domain of human investment (from 12 per cent to 18 per cent). Of the two major programmes under human investment, education was by far the largest, costing about $78 billion in 1975, compared to $17 billion allotted to health and medical programmes in the same year. The education programmes were financed and administered mainly by state and local governments.

While human investment (i.e. public investment in human capital) was intended to enhance the earning capacity of the population by raising the general standards of education and health, public income maintenance programmes were designed to make up for the loss of income due to various contingencies or for the lack of or deficiency in income up to a certain level. Both were expected to have an effect on poverty alleviation, but there was a clear distinction. The effects of human investment on poverty would be felt only after a long lapse of time and would be difficult to evaluate. Besides, many felt that the effectiveness of human investment as an anti-poverty instrument was open to question. Income maintenance programmes, on the other hand, had a direct and immediate impact on poverty alleviation, even though it is beyond their province to root out the causes of poverty.

Cash transfers and non-cash (in-kind) transfers. Among the great variety of public income maintenance programmes it is important to distinguish between cash transfers and non-cash (in-kind) transfers. The recipients of cash transfers were more or less free to spend the cash benefits in the manner they desired. The major cash transfer programmes were social insurance, the cash components of public-aid programmes and veteran's pension and compensation. Under non-cash or in-kind transfer programmes, most of which aimed to provide relief to the poor, the public payment was tied to a particular essential item of consumption. Among these items were food, medical assistance and housing for the needy, and various non-cash elements specified in the veteran's programmes. Public cash transfer programmes assumed a predominant role in the income maintenance expenditure. However, non-cash transfers had been expanding much more rapidly than cash transfers especially since the latter part of the sixties owing primarily to the great increases in food and medical assistance. By 1975 non-cash transfers had grown to 18.5 per cent of the total income maintenance expenditure compared to 7 per cent in 1965. Of particular significance was the complex relationship between cash and non-cash transfers which, as will be explained later, was becoming one of the main defects of the existing welfare system.

Specific and non-specific programmes. From the point of view of poverty alleviation the most significant feature of the public income maintenance expenditures was the predominance of specific programmes which by design provide benefits only to certain specific groups of population. Table II.5 gives a classification of income maintenance programmes including both cash and non-cash transfers by type of recipients for the period 1950-75. Roughly 90 per cent of the total income maintenance expenditure was allotted to population in five categories: the aged and survivors, the disabled (including the blind), veterans, the unemployed and female-headed families with dependent children. Despite the rapid growth in the total income maintenance expenditure, this proportion remained virtually unchanged over the last quarter of the century.

The lion's share went to the aged (65 years and over), the survivors, the disabled and the blind. As a group they absorbed over 60 per cent of the total income maintenance expenditure. The benefits paid to this group came primarily from social insurance but partly also from public aid provided since 1974 under the Federal Supplemental Security Income (SSI) Programme which superseded public assistance to the aged, blind and disabled. Ranked next were veterans' programmes which in the 1970s accounted for about 9 to 10 per cent of the total. The amount of unemployment benefits, which were mostly paid out of state unemployment insurance, varied each year with the rate of unemployment. In 1975 with a substantial increase in unemployment its relative importance in the total rose from 4.4 per cent in 1974 to 7.7 per cent. Unlike the programmes mentioned above which benefited the non-poor as well as the poor, aid to families with dependent children (AFDC) was designed explicitly to provide cash subsidy to families with dependent children in poverty but was, in practice, confined principally to families with dependent children headed by women. As a proportion of the total income expenditure in the 1970s the AFDC programme, which was federal-state jointly financed but administered by the state, represented about 5 to 6 per cent. Lastly, medicaid, as distinct from the health insurance for the aged (medicare), was fast expanding into another major federal-state jointly financed categorical programme. The beneficiaries of medicaid were restricted to the recipients of specific cash assistance under SSI and AFDC (i.e. the aged, disabled, blind and female-headed families with dependent children) and those in the same categories whose income minus medical expenses was less than 133 per cent of the needs standard in the state in question for cash assistance (the medically indigent). In the 1970s medicaid formed about 7 per cent of the total.

With the bulk (roughly 90 per cent) of the total income maintenance expenditure allotted to persons in the categories described above, only some 10 per cent of the total was left for the rest of the population in pre-transfer poverty. The rest consisted chiefly of "the working poor" - that is, families headed by able-bodied non-aged males who worked but whose earnings from employment were too low to lift their families over the poverty line; able-bodied non-aged childless couples and unrelated individuals of both sexes whose earnings were similarly

Table II.5 Income Maintenance Programmes by Type of Recipients in Selected Fiscal Years, 1950-1975
(Amount in billions of current dollars)

Year	Total income maintenance expenditure (in billions of current dollars)		Income maintenance programmes for five categories of population									...
			Aged and Disabled						Veterans		AFDC	...
			Social security (OASDHI)		OA, AB, APTD and SSI		Total					
	Amount	% of total	Amount	% of total	Amount	% of total	Amount	% of total	Amount	% of total	Amount	% of total ...
1950	14.7	100	2.6	17.7	1.5	10.2	4.1	27.9	6.7	45.6	0.5	3.4
1955	18.2	100	7.5	41.2	1.7	9.3	9.2	50.5	4.9	26.9	0.6	3.3
1960	29.7	100	16.2	54.5	1.9	6.4	18.1	60.9	5.5	18.5	1.0	3.4
1965	42.3	100	25.0	59.1	2.1	5.0	27.1	64.1	6.0	14.2	1.6	3.8
1970	84.7	100	50.7	59.9	2.9	3.4	53.6	63.3	9.1	10.7	4.9	5.8
1972	116.1	100	67.0	57.7	3.4	2.9	70.4	60.6	11.5	9.9	7.1	6.1
1973	132.2	100	80.0	60.5	3.4	2.6	83.4	63.1	13.0	9.8	7.3	5.5
1974	152.4	100	92.3	60.6	5.2	3.4	97.5	64.0	14.0	9.3	8.0	5.2
1975[1]	188.1	100	109.1	58.0	5.9	3.1	115.0	61.1	16.7	8.9	9.2	4.9

Source: see table II.3

1 Preliminary estimates.

Table II.5 (contd.)

	Income maintenance programmes for five categories of population						Other income maintenance programmes							
	Medicaid		Unemployment insurance		Total for five categories		General assistance		Food stamps		Other social welfare programmes		Total of other programmes	
Year	Amount	% of total	Amount	% of total	Amount	% of total	Amount	% of total	Amount	% of total	Amount	% of total	Amount	% of total
1950			2.3	15.6	13.6	92.5	0.3	2			0.8	5.4	1.1	7.5
1955			2.3	12.6	17.0	93.4	0.2	1.1			1.0	5.5	1.2	6.6
1960			3.1	10.9	27.7	93.3	0.3	1.0			1.7	5.7	2.0	6.7
1965			3.1	7.3	37.8	89.4	0.3	0.7	0.04	0.1	4.2	9.9	4.5	10.6
1970	5.2	6.1	3.9	4.6	76.7	90.6	0.6	0.7	0.60	0.7	6.8	8.0	8.0	9.4
1972	7.8	6.7	7.8	6.7	104.6	90.1	0.7	0.6	1.9	1.6	8.9	7.7	11.5	9.9
1973	9.2	7.0	6.1	4.6	119.0	90.0	0.7	0.5	2.2	1.7	10.3	7.8	13.2	10.0
1974	10.3	6.8	6.6	4.3	136.5	89.6	0.8	0.5	2.8	1.8	12.3	8.1	15.9	10.4
1975[1]	13.0	6.9	14.4	7.7	168.3	89.5	1.1	0.6	4.7	2.5	14.0	7.4	19.8	10.5

below the poverty line. In addition, there were the unemployed and, more especially, those without dependent children, who fell below the poverty line and were not eligible for unemployment benefits because they had already exhausted them.[1]

According to the crude classification used here, as is shown in table II.5, in 1975 the remaining 10.5 per cent of the total was made up as follows: 7.4 per cent went to "other social welfare" programmes, 2.5 per cent to food stamp programmes and 0.6 per cent to general assistance programmes. The "other social welfare" programmes, the largest of the three items, comprised a great number of diverse programmes at different government levels, such as public and subsidised housing, child nutrition and vocational rehabilitation.[2] Though they all had a poverty alleviation effect, programmes in this group were either limited in scale or specific in coverage. General assistance and food stamps, on the other hand, were non-specific and universally available to low-income families and individuals. These two were practically the only types of programmes to which the working poor and other excluded poor could turn for income support after passing the means test. The general assistance programmes were mainly cash transfer programmes financed and administered by state and local governments. The food stamp programme was essentially a federal programme of food subsidy to low-income households, the amount of subsidy varying directly with the size of the household and inversely with its income. Besides the working poor and other excluded poor, the recipients of AFDC and other cash assistance were automatically eligible for food stamps. Thus, when food stamps and general assistance were put together, no more than 3 per cent of the total income maintenance expenditure was available for general income support to the working poor and other excluded poor in 1975. Out of a total of 188.1 billion dollars (in current dollars) of income maintenance expenditure less than 4.8 billion (since part of the food stamp expenditure is shared by specific cash assistance recipients) went to the working poor and other excluded poor compared to 168.3 billion allotted to the aged, survivors, disabled, veterans and female-headed families with dependent children.

The effects of three major cash transfer programmes on poverty

It would be pertinent to ascertain how far the income maintenance (cash and non-cash) expenditures distributed in the manner described above had actually alleviated the poverty of different groups of population. An adequate analysis of their effects is hindered by the use of cash income including transfer

---

[1] In many states the unemployed with dependent children who were not eligible for unemployment compensation were entitled to the AFDC-UF Programme (UF stands for unemployed father).

[2] In addition to those already mentioned, this group included, among others, work-experience training programmes under the Economic Opportunity Act and the Comprehensive Employment and Training Act, Indian welfare and guidance, aging and juvenile delinquency activities, work relief, other emergency aid, repatriate and refugee assistance, amounts of anti-poverty and manpower programmes from state and local funds. Action and special Office of Economic Opportunity (OEO) programmes such as community action and migrant workers.

income as the income measure in the available poverty statistics. Nevertheless, a limited attempt was made to compare the changes in the number of post-transfer population below the official poverty line classified into four groups with the changes in the amount (in constant 1975 dollars) of cash payment under the corresponding cash transfer programmes to the benefit of which each group was entitled over the period 1966-75. The classification is as follows:

Groups below the poverty line	The corresponding cash transfer programmes
65 years and over	Retirement (including survivors and dependants) cash benefits payment (not including veterans)
Persons in female-headed families below 65 years	AFDC
Persons in male-headed families below 65 years Unrelated individuals below 65 years	General assistance

The two sets of corresponding figures by this rough classification arc presented in table II.6. A comparison of these figures brings out several findings which are briefly discussed below.

1. A striking disproportion can be discerned between the percentage distribution of the poor among the four groups and that of the cash transfer expenditure among the three types of programmes. Retirement cash benefits payment absorbed nearly 93 per cent of the total cash transfers of the three types of programmes combined in 1966 and declined moderately to 89 per cent in 1975. On the other hand, the aged (65 years and over) as a group formed about 20 per cent of the poverty population in 1966 and 13 per cent in 1975. In glaring contrast, the non-aged (below 65 years) persons in male-headed families and unrelated individuals combined as a group, constituted 59 per cent of the poverty population in 1966 and 54 per cent in 1975. The amount of cash transfer available to them under general assistance programmes remained at approximately one per cent of the total cash transfers of the three types combined. Between the two extremes was the position of non-aged persons in female-headed families. The latter represented 23 per cent of the poverty population in 1966 and rose to 33 per cent in 1975, whereas the amount of AFDC was only 6.5 per cent of the combined cash transfers in 1966 but increased to 10 per cent in 1975.

Table II.6 Three Major Types of Cash Transfer Programmes and the Corresponding Types of Recipients: A Comparison in Distribution and Changes in Size (Number of Persons in thousands. Amount in millions of constant 1975 dollars.)

	Total number of persons below poverty line	Total amount of the three types of cash transfer programmes	65 years and over		Below 65 years of age					
					Persons in female-headed families					
			Changes in number below poverty line	Changes in overall retirement cash payment[1]	Changes in number below poverty line	Changes in AFDC payment	Changes in number of persons in male-headed families below poverty line (A)	Changes in number of unrelated individuals below poverty line (B)	Changes in A + B	Changes in general assistance payments
1966 level										
total figure	28 510	$46 999	5 114	$43 513	6 501	$3 068	14 801	2 094	16 895	$418
% distribution	100%	100%	17.9%	92.6%	22.8%	6.5%	51.9%	7.3%	59.2%	0.9%
1966-69	- 4 363	+ 9 935	- 219	+ 7 537	- 10	+ 2 120	- 4 303	+ 168	- 4 135	+ 278
1969-71	+ 1 412	+13 227	- 622	+ 9 814	+ 979	+ 3 097	+ 727	+ 325	+ 1 052	+ 316
1971-73	- 2 586	+13 582	- 919	+13 218	+ 439	+ 543	- 2 175	+ 72	- 2 103	- 179
1973-74[2]	+ 1 287	+ 3 219	- 46	+ 3 255	+ 446	- 104	+ 792	+ 95	+ 887	+ 68
1974[3]-75	+ 2 507	+ 6 379	+ 232	+ 5 657	+ 393	+ 486	+ 1 499	+ 384	+ 1 883	+ 236
Cumulative change 1966-75	- 1 743	+46 342	-1 574	+39 481	+2 247	+ 6 142	- 3 460	+1 044	- 2 416	+ 719
1975 level total figures	25 877	93 341	3 317	82 994	8 657	9 210	10 941	2 963	13 904	1 137
% distribution	100%	100%	12.8%	88.9%	33.5%	9.9%	42.3%	11.4%	53.7%	1.2%

Source: Figures for amounts of the three major types of cash transfer programmes from table II.3. Figures for number of persons 65 years old and over and below 65 years of age computed from data given in various issues of Bureau of Census' annual reports on Characteristics of low-income population and on money income and poverty status of persons in the United States, quoted earlier.

[1] Total sum of cash benefits payments under Old-age and Survivors Insurance plus OAA or SSI to the aged plus public and railroad employee retirement cash benefits payment.

[2] Unrevised figure for 1974.

[3] Revised figure for 1974.

2. The enormous absolute and relative size of retirement cash payment is easily explained. As already indicated, aside from public assistance to the aged (formerly OAA and since 1974, SSI), the payment was made both to the poor and the non-poor out of social insurance. Hence, it would be misleading to compare the size of retirement payment to the size of AFDC and general assistance, since the latter types were designed only for assisting the poor. None the less, as can be seen from table II.6, the successive increases in aggregate retirement payments over the period were accompanied by successive decreases in the number of the aged below the official poverty line (except for the recession year 1975). Between 1966 and 1974 the number fell from 5.1 million to 3.3 million or by 1.8 million and the poverty incidence among the aged from 28.5 per cent to 15.7 per cent. This substantial decrease in the number of aged poor can be ascribed almost wholly to the some $40 billion (in constant 1975 dollars) increase in retirement payments, even though a good portion of it went to the non-poor. In comparison with other groups of the poor, the aged appear to have been the most favoured from the point of view of anti-poverty policy.

3. In the case of non-aged persons in female-headed families while the amount of AFDC payment increased threefold from about $3.1 billion (in constant 1975 dollars) in 1966 to $9.2 billion in 1975, the number of persons in poverty, however, continued to increase over the period from 6.5 million to 8.7 million. The high poverty incidence among this group declined only slightly from 42 to 39 per cent. As a proportion of total population, non-aged persons in female-headed families represented only 8 per cent in 1966 and 10 per cent in 1975. Thus, the growth of AFDC by itself, rapid as it was, did not prove sufficient to keep this expanding group of the poor from rising in absolute number after cash transfer.

4. General assistance programmes seem to have had little effect on the number of non-aged persons in male-headed families below the poverty line nor on the number of poor unrelated individuals. Among non-aged persons in male-headed families the number below the poverty line was governed primarily by the changes in economic conditions. As is shown in table II.6, the number decreased considerably during 1966-69 when unemployment was relatively low (3.5 to 3.8 per cent) and during 1971-73 when the growth rate of GNP was fairly high (5.3 to 5.8 per cent). Conversely, the increase in number during 1966-71 was associated with an economic recession, and more markedly so during the latest recession of 1974-75. Over the period 1966-75 the number of non-aged persons in male-headed families fell from 14.8 million to about 11 million or by some 4 million, and the poverty incidence from 9.6 to 7 per cent. The decrease, however, could be attributed only marginally to income support from general assistance programmes. As regards non-aged unrelated individuals, the number in poverty rose steadily over the period from 2 million to some 3 million. For them, the beneficial effect of general assistance also appears to have been minimal.

As pointed out earlier, the data on the number and distribution of the poverty population used in the above comparison with cash transfer expenditures refer to persons in post-transfer poverty. For a more meaningful comparison the data used should be for the pre-transfer poverty population. Such data were not regularly available. However, some writers have made attempts to estimate the effects of income maintenance expenditures in taking people out of pre-transfer poverty. Some of their estimates are considered later in this chapter.

The major anti-poverty programmes

The foregoing overview of public social welfare expenditures placed in perspective the various types of these expenditures in relation to different groups of the poverty population. This section proceeds to a more substantive review of the major income maintenance programmes. These are OASDHI (social security) and unemployment insurance under social insurance together with Supplemental Security Income; and medicaid and food stamps under public assistance. In addition, public sector employment programmes as a means of poverty alleviation will be discussed.

Social insurance

Social insurance as originally conceived in the Social Security Act of 1935 aimed primarily at the protection of families or individuals against loss of earnings due to certain specified contingencies in life regardless of whether the insured was rich or poor. The contingencies had been extended with the amendments of the Act. By the 1970s, social insurance as commonly understood in the United States consisted of two distinct types: the old-age, survivors, disability and health insurance for the aged - collectively known as social security or OASDHI, and unemployment insurance. Since social insurance was originally based on the principle of replacement of lost earnings, the benefits conferred on an insured person varied directly with his past earnings and these amounted to only a proportion of his current earnings. The lowest paid workers usually received the least benefits. The arrangement under social insurance was thus unfavourable to the poor. This deficiency had long been recognised and remedial measures were taken through sucessive legislative action.

OASDHI. The old-age, survivors, and disability and medicare programme was the largest single income transfer programme in the United States. Between 1970 and 1975 the number of recipients under OASDHI programme increased by 22 per cent. In 1975 the programme covered 32 million persons or about 90 per cent of all wage and salary earners and the self-employed, not including federal civil employees who were under a separate federal retirement programme.[1] The coverage of OASDHI, as of the beginning of 1975, excluded casual agricultural and domestic employment, and had a limited coverage of self-employment (when annual net income is below $400).[2] Ever since 1939 the programme had been broadened steadily into a family programme by addition of benefits for dependants (wives and children) and survivors. Thus, it was estimated that by the 1970s "one of three social security cheques

---

[1] Economic Report of the President Transmitted to the Congress, January 1976 (Washington, D.C., 1976), pp. 111-112.

[2] US Department of Health, Education and Welfare, Social Security Administration: Social Security Programme Throughout the World, 1975 (Washington, D.C. 1976), p. 236.

goes to persons under 65 years of age, including about three million children".[1]

Under OASDHI the amount of a worker's basic monthly benefit was calculated on the basis of the worker's record of covered earnings over a specified number of years. For retirement benefits, the period was 20 years. The amount of dependants' supplement depended on the benefit level of the primary beneficiary.[2]

One notable change in OASDHI over the past decades was a progressive shift from the earnings replacement principle to the needs-based principle. The broadening into a family programme referred to above was only one aspect of this change. The other aspect was the raising of the replacement rates (i.e. the ratio of benefits to previous earnings) used in the benefit formula increasingly in favour of low earners so that they were entitled to greater benefits relative to their previous earnings than higher earners. According to one study, the ratio of maximum benefits to minimum benefit paid to a retired worker had fallen from 8.5 times as provided by the law in 1935 to 4 times in 1950 and 3.2 times in July 1974.[3]

Between 1970 and 1975 the average monthly benefit for retired workers in real terms increased by 26 per cent.[4] In 1975, OASDHI benefit levels were automatically adjusted to changes in the cost of living. As of January 1976, OASDHI benefits were financed by a payroll tax of 9.9 per cent levied on the first $15,300 of wages. This was the maximum taxable earnings base and the latter

---

[1] US 93rd Congress, 2nd Session: Joint Committee Print: Income Security for Americans: Recommendations of the Public Welfare Study: Report of the Sub-committee on Fiscal Policy of the Joint Economic Committee, Congress of the United States, Together with Supplementary views (Washington, D.C. 5 Dec. 1974), p. 34.

[2] As of the beginning of 1975, for old-age pension (retirement benefit) the qualifying conditions were: age 65 (age 62-65 with reduction). Insured: at least one-quarter of coverage (QC) for each year since 1950 to age 62; maximum, 40 QC. Pension reduced $1 for each $2 of earnings above $2,520 a year until age 72. The old-age pension for a retired worker was based on covered earnings after 1950 up to retirement age or death (excluding 5 lowest years). For dependants' allowance: 50 per cent of worker's pension to wife or dependent husband age 65 (reduced for 62-65) or to wife at any age caring for child under 18 or invalid; to each child (or dependent grandchild) under 18 (22 if student, no age limit if invalid before age 22). As of the beginning of 1975, old-age pensions: minimum, $93.30 a month, maximum $316.30; family pension: minimum, $140.80 a month, maximum, $573.90. (US Department of Health, Education and Welfare, Social Security Administration: Social Security Programmes Throughout the World, 1975, op. cit., pp. 236-237.)

[3] US 93rd Congress, 2nd Session: Joint Committee Print: Income Security for Americans: Recommendations of the Public Welfare Study, op. cit., p. 35.

[4] Economic Report of the President Transmitted to Congress, 1975, op. cit., p. 111.

was linked to changes in the average of covered wages.[1] The payroll tax was shared equally by employers and employees. Rising benefits for retired workers and their dependants were thus, in reality paid by workers who were currently working. Even the part paid by employers was at least partially paid by current workers, since it was most likely shifted backwards to the workers by reducing wages and/or forwards to the consumers by rising prices. Furthermore, the payroll tax levied for this purpose was a regressive tax because of the ceiling on taxable earnings, and the burden of this tax at 9.9 per cent was particularly heavy on low-wage workers.

Despite the raising of OASDHI benefits, the average level of benefits in 1975 was still low in relation to the corresponding poverty line income. In December 1975, the average monthly benefit for retired workers amounted to $207.18, and that for dependent wives and husbands, $105.19.[2] These two payments combined might be taken roughly as the family pension for a two-person family headed by a male of 65 years and over without dependent children. The combined sum was $312.37 a month or $3,778 a year. This annual sum was only 15 per cent (or $488) above the poverty line income for a two-person family of the same description ($3,260) in 1975.[3] Though data on the dispersion of benefit levels were not readily available, there can be little doubt that large numbers of retired workers received benefits below the average level. In the absence of other sources of income or savings, these retired workers would fall below the poverty line. The minimum monthly benefit to persons retiring at the beginning of 1975 at age 65 was $101 in June 1975, whereas the maximum monthly benefit to men retiring at age 65 was $342 and that to women, $362.[4] A two-person family living on the minimum retirement benefit would have an annual family pension of $1,818 (= $101 times 1.5 times 12) or no more than 56 per cent of the corresponding poverty line income in 1975. It is also of interest to note that even at the maximum retirement benefit the family pension for a two-person family would be less than twice the corresponding poverty line income.

---

[1] The self-employed paid a tax of 7 per cent. An additional tax of 1.8 per cent for wage and salary workers and 0.9 per cent for the self-employed was for medicare hospital insurance for the aged. (ibid., p. 112.)

[2] US Department of Health, Education and Welfare, Social Security Administration: Social Security Bulletin, Vol. 29, No. 11, Nov. 1976, table M-13, p. 62.

[3] Figure from US Department of Commerce, Bureau of the Census: Money Income and Poverty Status of Families and Persons in the United States: 1975 and 1974 Revisions (Advance Report), op. cit. p. 33.

[4] Economic Report of the President Transmitted to the Congress, January 1976, p. 112.

The low level of retirement benefits was due chiefly to the use of average covered earnings of the recipient as the benefit base for two reasons. First, over the 20 years that were taken into account normally his or her earnings in the year before retirement were bound to be much higher than the 20-year average. Second, since the calculations were based only on past money earnings, the fall in their real value with rising consumer prices was not taken into consideration. The automatic adjustment of benefits to changes in consumer prices was clearly an important improvement but it did not cover the reduced real value of the past earnings. The latter, however, had been redressed, at least in part, by the substantial raising of the benefit level during the 1970s.

The raising of the benefit level did improve the size of benefit in relation to the poverty level. By the same method of comparison as used above the family pension at the average benefit level for a two-person family headed by a male of 65 years without dependent children was found to be about 80 per cent of the corresponding poverty line income in 1965 and 82 per cent in 1969. Only since 1971 did it finally reach and then exceed the poverty line income.[1] Thus, measured by poverty line income, between 1969 and 1975 the benefit level increased by approximately 40 per cent, even though the level was still relatively low.

The considerable increase in retirement benefits was a main factor in lifting great numbers of families headed by retired workers over the poverty line during the period 1969-1974. Another factor was the replacement of the three state-administered (with federal financial participation) public assistance programmes for the aged, disabled and blind by the federal supplemental security income (SSI) programme since 1974. As a supplement to OASDHI, SSI provided a nationally uniform cash income floor for the aged, disabled and blind. As of July 1974 the SSI guarantee was $146 per person and $219 per couple per month with a 50 per cent benefit reduction rate for earnings from work (after an initial exemption of $85 of monthly earnings).[2] This newly established federal programme should be expected to have a positive effect on poverty alleviation.

---

[1] The average monthly benefits for retired workers and for dependent wives and husbands in 1965, and 1969 to 1975 used in this comparison were taken from US Department of Health, Education and Welfare, Social Security Administration: Social Security Bulletin, Vol. 39, No. 11, Nov. 1976, table M-13, p. 62; the corresponding poverty line incomes for 1972-75 were taken from US Department of Commerce, Bureau of the Census: Current Population Report, Characteristics of the Low-income Population, 1972; Characteristics of the Low-income Population 1973; Money Income and Poverty Status of Families and Persons in the United States 1974 and 1975 (Advance Reports); those for 1965 and 1969 were obtained by applying a ratio of 0.5927 to the average poverty line income for a non-farm family of four persons given in Characteristics of the Low-income Population, 1973.

[2] US 93rd Congress, 2nd Session: Joint Committee Print: Income Security for Americans: Recommendations of the Public Welfare Study, op. cit., p. 41.

Unemployment insurance. Unemployment insurance in the United States was run mainly by the States with the aid of federal guidelines.[1] Benefits were funded from a payroll tax levied on employers in proportion to workers' base wages.[2] As of January 1975, the basic tax rate was 2.7 per cent of the payroll. The actual rate varied according to individual employers' unemployment experience rating based on the extent to which their workers drew benefits from state unemployment insurance. The average rate in 1974 was about 2 per cent.[3] In addition, employers paid a federal tax of 0.5 per cent.

The effectiveness of the state unemployment insurance programmes in alleviating poverty among the unemployed was determined by its coverage, its eligibility requirements, the amount of benefits received by the unemployed and the duration of payment. With the onset of the 1974-75 recession and the attendant high rate of unemployment, in December 1974 Congress enacted emergency unemployment compensation legislation to enable Federal Government to mitigate the impact of rising unemployment by liberalising some of these restraints.

According to federal law, the regular state unemployment insurance programmes covered firms in industry, commerce and non-profit institutions with four or more employees during 20 weeks in a year. Four-fifths of the states covered state or local government employees. The exclusions were: agricultural employees, domestic servants, employees of religious organisations, casual employees, family labour, self-employed, and state or local government employees in one-fifth of states.[4] With these important categories of exclusion, a large number of workers fell outside state unemployment insurance. In January 1975, pursuant to the Emergency Jobs and Unemployment Assistance Act passed by the Congress in December 1974, a temporary federally funded special unemployment assistance (SUA) programme was introduced to provide benefits for wage and salary workers not covered by a regular federal or state programme. As a result, coverage was extended to about 12 million additional wage and salary workers in 1975. Only 8 million self-employed and unpaid workers remained uncovered.[5]

---

[1] In addition, Federal Government had direct federal unemployment programmes covering four special groups: railroad workers, recently discharged members of the Armed Forces, federal civilian employees and those unemployed as a consequence of imports. (Economic Report of the President Transmitted to the Congress, January 1976, op. cit., p. 106.)

[2] Workers' base wages in 1976 were equal in most states to the first $4,200. (Economic Report of the President Transmitted to the Congress, January 1976, op. cit., p. 108.)

[3] US Department of Health, Education and Welfare, Social Security Administration: Social Security Programmes Throughout the World, 1975, op. cit., p. 236.

[4] US Department of Health, Education and Welfare, Social Security Administration: Social Security Programmes Throughout the World, 1975, op. cit., p. 236.

[5] Economic Report of the President Transmitted to the Congress, January 1976, op. cit., p. 108.

As regards eligibility requirements, though they varied under different state rules, "generally, to be eligible for benefits a person must have had sufficient work experience and earnings in covered employment in a recent one-year period prior to the onset of unemployment. As a result of the work experience requirements, new entrants and most re-entrants to the labour force do not qualify for benefits."[1] To aid recent entrants under the Emergency Jobs and Unemployment Assistance Act of 1974 the use of the most recent 52 weeks was adopted for satisfying the employment requirement to replace the usual practice of using the 52 weeks prior to the most recent three-month period.[2] Other eligibility requirements were ability to work, availability and readinesss for work and registration at employment services. The law further provided that benefits were payable to insured persons, unemployed but not due to voluntarily leaving, misconduct, labour dispute, or refusal of a suitable offer.

Under the regular state unemployment insurance programmes the duration of benefit entitlement increased with the amount of work experience during the base period in 43 states, generally up to a 26-week ceiling. In the other seven states the state rule provided a fixed duration for all the recipients of unemployment benefits. In times of high state or national unemployment, a 1970 law permanently authorised an extension of benefits to 39 weeks. In 1975 federal law provided for a further temporary extension in all states by an additional 26 weeks in time of high unemployment to a maximum duration of 65 weeks. The benefits for the additional 26 weeks were paid under federal supplemental benefits (FSB) out of general revenues.[3] Under the federal special unemployment assistance programme (SUA), however, benefits for some workers ineligible for the regular state and federal programmes lasted up to 26 weeks.[4] Strikingly enough, despite the further extension of duration of benefit entitlement under FSB, "the rise in the unemployment rate was accompanied by an increase in the number of persons who exhausted their

---

[1] <u>Economic Report of the President Transmitted to the Congress January 1976</u>, op. cit., p. 107. As of January 1975, almost three-quarters of states required minimum earnings in preceding base year equal to specified multiple of weekly benefit or high-quarter wages, or to specified total amount. Fourteen states required a specified number of weeks (e.g. 14-20 weeks). (See US Department of Health, Education and Welfare, Social Security Administration: <u>Social Security Programmes Throughout the World, 1975</u>, p. 236.)

[2] <u>Economic Report of the President Transmitted to the Congress, 1975</u> (Washington D.C. 1975), p. 120.

[3] <u>Economic Report of the President Transmitted to the Congress, 1976</u>, op. cit., p. 109.

[4] <u>Economic Report of the President Transmitted to the Congress, February 1975</u>, op. cit., p. 120.

unemployment benefits from about 2.0 million in 1974 to 4.3 million in 1975."[1] This doubling of exhaustion of unemployment benefits was considered one of the main reasons for the 10.7 per cent increase in the number of families (from 4.9 to 5.5 million) below the poverty line from 1974 to 1975.[2]

In 43 states weekly unemployment benefits were about 50 per cent of the workers' pre-tax wage up to a ceiling that varied among the states from $60 per week in Indiana to $139 per week in the District of Columbia as of January 1976.[3] Data on minimum benefits for the same period were not available, but earlier data showed that minimum basic weekly benefits in different states were exceedingly low.[4] Twelve states supplemented the unemployed worker's benefit with a small dependency allowance for a spouse or dependent children who were not working.

The average weekly benefit for total unemployment under state programmes in 1975 was $70.23 including dependant allowances in states which provided such benefits.[5] Converted into an annual income the average unemployment benefit in 1975 would amount to $3 652 in current dollars. This amount was equivalent to 66 per cent of the poverty line income for a non-farm four-person family ($5,500), 85 per cent of that for a non-farm three-person family ($4,293), and about 100 per cent of that for a non-farm two-person family with a male head below 65 years of age ($3,636). Measured by the poverty line, the average unemployment benefit was, therefore, quite low - lower than the average benefit under OASDHI. Furthermore, unlike OASDHI the ratio of average unemployment benefit to poverty line income did not

---

[1] US Department of Commerce, Bureau of the Census: Money Income and Poverty Status of Families and Persons in the United States: 1975 and 1974 Revisions (Advance Report), op. cit., p.1.

[2] Op. cit., pp. 2-3.

[3] Economic Report of the President Transmitted to the Congress, January 1976, op. cit., p. 107.

[4] The report on Social Security Programmes Throughout the World, 1975 gave the following figures on weekly unemployment benefits in the United States: minimum basic weekly benefit: $5 to $30 (4/5 of states, $12 or more). Maximum, $60 ($50 in Puerto Rico) to $127 (1/2 states, $83 or more) according to the state. Average benefit was $59 a week. (US Department of Health, Education and Welfare, Social Security Administration: Social Security Programmes Throughout the World, 1975, op. cit., p. 237.) It was not clear as to which year these figures refer to although the report on the whole covered data at the beginning of 1975.

[5] US Department of Health, Education and Welfare, Social Security Administration: Social Security Bulletin, Vol. 39, No. 11, Nov. 1976, table M-37, p. 79.

show any significant rising trend during the 1970s.[1] It seems that those unemployed workers whose wages were less than twice their respective poverty line income would sink below the poverty line if living entirely on the unemployment benefit without savings or incomes from any other sources. True, unemployment compensation was meant only to tide the unemployed over a period of temporary unemployment. But during that period the low wage earner would have to endure living below the minimum subsistence standard even with his unemployment benefit. If, by the time their unemployment benefits were exhausted they remained unemployed, their living conditions would fall further. In view of the plight of low-wage earners who were unemployed, the Supreme Court in June 1975 took a decision which allows unemployed fathers in low-income families to accept AFDC-UF benefits instead of unemployment compensation.[2] AFDC-UF would provide them with larger benefits but also had certain unsatisfactory features which will be discussed presently.

The foregoing analysis has led to the following observations on the effect of unemployment insurance on poverty alleviation especially during the 1974-75 recession:

1. The broadening of coverage to include wage and salary workers not covered by the regular state and federal programmes under the federal special unemployment assistance (SUA) programme and the extension of the duration of benefit entitlement to a maximum of 65 weeks under federal supplemental benefits (FSB) programme - both introduced in January 1975 - had undoubtedly kept large numbers of unemployed above the poverty line. They would have fallen below the poverty line in the absence of these new federal programmes. However, both the SUA programme and the FSB programme were temporary measures. Under the legislation prevailing at the beginning of 1976 both programmes were scheduled to terminate in March 1977.[3]

---

[1] The ratios were computed from figures of average weekly unemployment benefit given in Social Security Bulletin, Vol. 39, 11 Nov. 1976, loc. cit., p. 79; and figures for poverty line income for a non-farm four-person family were given in US Department of Commerce: Characteristics of the Low-Income Population: 1973, op. cit., p. 160 and in US Department of Commerce: Money Income and Poverty Status of Families and Persons in the United States: 1974 (Advance Report), op. cit., p. 16, and Money Income and Poverty Status of Families in the United States: 1975 and 1974 Revisions (Advance Report) op. cit. p. 33.

[2] Economic Report of the President Transmitted to the Congress, January 1976, op. cit., p. 108.

[3] Economic Report of the President Transmitted to the Congress, January 1976, op. cit., p. 109.

2. On the other hand, the effectiveness of unemployment insurance in alleviating poverty was reduced by the eligibility requirements and by the low level of unemployment benefits. Because of the work experience requirement, new entrants and recent re-entrants to the labour force did not qualify for unemployment benefits. These included, in particular, unemployed youths and women whose unemployment rates were much higher than the average. The "discouraged workers" who had ceased to actively look for a job because jobs were unavailable, were also ineligible for unemployment benefits. Among the unemployed receiving unemployment benefits the low-wage workers, when unemployed, would suffer a cut in their already meagre standard of living because of the small amount of benefits they were entitled to.

Aid to families with dependent children

In the 1935 Social Security Act public assistance comprising aid to families with dependent children (AFDC) and aid to the aged, blind and disabled was treated as a supplement to social insurance. Its original purpose was to provide income support to the needy who were either ineligible for social insurance benefits or whose benefits were too low to meet their minimum needs.

Public assistance programmes were put into operation on principles quite different from the original principles underlying social insurance programmes. First, whereas social insurance required a contribution paid into the insurance trust by the beneficiaries or by their employers, public assistance was to be financed wholly from public funds. Second, whereas under social insurance the amount of benefit varied directly with the beneficiary's previous earnings, under public assistance the amount of benefit varied inversely with the beneficiary's current income. Third, whereas the participants of social insurance, rich or poor, were entitled to a benefit as a matter of right, the beneficiaries of public assistance, who were mostly either poor or near-poor, had to pass the means or income test before qualifying for the benefit. Fourth, whereas social insurance programmes were either directly administered by the Federal Government as in the case of OASDHI or under close federal supervision as in the case of unemployment insurance, the administration of, and the rules set for, public assistance programmes were left to the state governments under only general federal guidelines, though these programmes were mostly financed jointly by Federal and state and/or local governments. Lastly, at the time when the social security legislation was first enacted, it was expected that contrary to social insurance, public assistance would wither away in the course of time with the expansion of social insurance coverage and increase in its benefits and with the rise in the level of average income. The expectations, however, failed to be borne out by the subsequent developments. Instead of withering away, public assistance kept on expanding along with social insurance.

AFDC was a major component of public assistance or public welfare. It was designed to provide financial assistance, and social services as well, to families in which dependent children were deprived of support of a parent (usually the father) through death, disability or absence. The expansion of its coverage and increases in its benefits including simultaneous eligibility for in-kind benefits coupled with increases in poor families headed by women had brought about a rapid growth of the AFDC programme during the 1960s. AFDC families as a percentage of all female-headed families with children rose from 38.3 per cent in 1960 to 81.8 per cent in 1970 to the peak at 83.5 per cent in 1973, then fell to 77.1 per cent in 1975.[1] The number of AFDC recipients soared from 3.1 million in 1960, to 9.7 million in 1970 and to 11.4 million in 1975 or by 268 per cent over the period, while the total amount of AFDC cash payments increased correspondingly from about 1 billion to 4.9 billion and to 9.2 billion in current dollars or by 410 per cent in constant dollars over the period.[2] Accompanying this rapid growth in the number of AFDC recipients was a shift in the composition of recipients to families with absent fathers.[3]

Since AFDC was one of the major anti-poverty instruments, it would be of particular interest to assess their actual effect in reducing the poverty of its target population. While a quantitative assessment was not possible in the absence of pre-transfer data, certain features of AFDC bearing directly on its effectiveness in poverty alleviation are discussed below.

(a) Low maximum payment standards and wide inter-state variations

For AFDC it was within the jurisdiction of each state to establish its own basic needs standard. An applicant whose income was below the needs standard was eligible for AFDC. While the needs standard was used to determine eligibility, states were not required by law to pay eligible families with no other income benefits actually at that level. Hence, in addition to their needs standards, many, but not all states set their maximum payment standard (in any case below their needs standards) from which the family's other incomes were subtracted to determine the amount of benefit to which the family is entitled. Moreover, states generally reimbursed recipients for certain work-related expenses, and, in some states certain other expenses as well. The items and amounts of such expenses to be covered were

---

[1] Economic Report of the President Transmitted to the Congress, January 1976, op. cit., p. 97. Data are for December of each year except 1975 which is for September. Data exclude families with unemployed fathers.

[2] US Department of Health, Education and Welfare, Social Security Administration: Social Security Bulletin, Vol. 29, No. 11, Nov. 1976, table M-32, p. 75 and table M.33, p. 76. Figures for number of AFDC recipients refer to December of each year.

[3] "By 1971 only 14 per cent of AFDC families were headed by widows or contained an incapacited man; 76 per cent were headed by women who were divorced, deserted, seperated, never married, otherwise living apart from their children's fathers; and the remaining 10 per cent were intact families, many were helped under a programme for unemployed fathers, first enacted in 1961." (Henry J. Aaron: Why Is Welfare So Hard to Reform? (The Brookings Institution, Washington, D.C., 1973), p. 7.)

usually left to the discretion of welfare workers. These and other differences in rules and practices gave rise to a wide inter-state variation in the level of payment and the proportion of families receiving AFDC benefits.

Wide inter-state variations notwithstanding, only in a few states did the maximum payment standards come near the official poverty line. The majority of states set their maximum payment standards substantially below the poverty line. In one recent study, states were ranked by the maximum AFDC payment standards for a penniless mother with three children in July 1974 as ratios to the corresponding official poverty line.[1] These are reproduced in table II.7 together with other relevant data. As can be seen, the maximum standard reached within 10 per cent below the poverty line in the top state and fell to as little as less than 20 per cent of the poverty line in the bottom state. On these ratios the study made the following observations:[2]

> The range between the top state (New York) and the bottom state (Mississippi) was nearly 7 to 1. About 23 per cent of the AFDC caseload received maximum cash support equivalent to less than 40 per cent of the poverty levels, 37 per cent of the caseload receives maximum support under 60 per cent of the poverty level. A privileged 29 per cent of the caseload receives support above 70 per cent of the poverty level. If the figures were weighted by the population of poor female-headed families with children in each state, instead of the AFDC caseloads, the picture would further emphasise the widespread extent of low-benefit levels.

Within the range shown above the lowest maximum AFDC payment standards were in the southern states where the poverty incidence was much higher, the poverty income gap wider, and where the larger portion of the Black poverty population was located. Regarding the regional imbalance in AFDC aid relative to the distribution of poverty population, the study referred to above found the following situation at the beginning of 1974:[3]

---

[1] 93rd US Congress, 2nd Session: Joint Economic Committee: Income Security For Americans: Recommendations of the Public Welfare Study: Report of the Sub-committee on Fiscal Policy, together with Supplementary Views (Washington, D.C. 5 Dec. 1974), p. 70.

[2] ibid., p. 69.

[3] 93rd US Congress, 2nd Session: Joint Economic Committee: Income Security for Americans: Recommendations of the Public Welfare Study, op. cit., p. 52.

Table II.7 State variations in AFDC maximum support levels for a penniless mother with three children, with and without food stamp bonus, weighted by AFDC caseload, 1974; and medicaid payments to families with dependent children, August 1973.

Ratio of support level to poverty threshold[1]	July 1974 maximum AFDC payments alone				July 1974 maximum AFDC payment plus allowable food stamp bonus[4]				August 1973 medicaid payments for families with dependent chldn. by States ranked in col.1	
	Number of States[2] (1)	Families receiving AFDC February 1974 (thousands)[3] (2)	Percent of all families (3)	Cumulative percent of all families (4)	Number of States (5)	Families receiving AFDC February 1974 (thousands) (6)	Percent of all families (7)	Cumulative percent of all families (8)	Medicaid vendor payments (millions)[5] (9)	Medicaid vendor payments divided by February 1974 AFDC caseload (col.9 ÷ col.2)[6] (10)
0.10 - 0.19	1	55	1.7	1.7	----	----	----	----	$ 1.4	$ 25.4
0.20 - 0.29	3	153	4.8	6.5	----	----	----	----	4.2	27.4
0.30 - 0.39	8	520	16.3	22.8	----	----	----	----	22.5	43.3
0.40 - 0.49	5	255	8.0	30.8	1	55	1.7	1.7	22.9	89.8
0.50 - 0.59	8	190	6.0	36.8	6	282	8.9	10.6	10.1	53.1
0.60 - 0.69	6	331	10.4	47.2	7	480	15.1	25.7	28.0	93.0
0.70 - 0.79	11	762	23.9	71.1	13	394	12.4	38.1	65.2	85.5
0.80 - 0.89	10	576	18.1	89.2	11	822	25.8	63.9	44.5	77.8
0.90 - 0.99	1	344	10.8	100.0	12	760	23.9	87.8	71.5	207.8
1.00 - 1.09	----	----	----	----	3	393	12.3	100.0	----	----
Total	53	3,186	100.0	100.0	53	3,186	100.0	100.0	270.1	85.8

<u>Source</u>: 93rd US Congress, 2nd Session: Joint Economic Committee: <u>Income Security for Americans: Recommendations of the Public Welfare Study</u>: Report of the Sub-committee on Fiscal Policy, 5 Dec. 1974 (US Government Printing Office, Washington, 1974), p. 70.

<u>Notes</u>: (See next page).

Notes to table II.7:

[1] Based on poverty threshold of $5,018 annually, which is the Census Bureau non-farm figure for a mother with three children in 1973, inflated by a cost-of-living increase of 11.4 per cent from the 1973 average price level to the level in July 1974.

[2] Unpublished data supplied by US Department of Health, Education and Welfare. To receive the maximum AFDC payments in most states, families had to pay at least the maximum amount of rent eligible for AFDC reimbursement in their area. In exceptional cases, actual maximum payments may exceed the figures used here. In the case of Michigan, the state maximum of $400 applies only in Ann Arbor, so the next highest level of $354 for Wayne County was used. In the case of New York City, rent payments can go as high as $300 or more, giving an AFDC monthly support level of $558 and above, so the Albany maximum rent of $153 was used, giving a monthly total of $411. The District of Colombia, Puerto Rico and the Virgin Islands are included in the tabulations.

[3] Data from US Department of Health, Education and Welfare, National Center for Social Statistics, "Recipients of Public Assistance Money Payments and Amounts of Such Payments by Program, State and County, Feb. 1974", Washington, 1974.

[4] Computed from food stamp schedules applicable starting July 1974.

[5] Data from "Medical Assistance (Medicaid) Financed under title XIX of the Social Security Act, August 1973". Data for Colorado and Alaska were not available, and Arizona had no programme.

[6] Adjustments were made to the AFDC caseload data to remove the caseloads of Colorado and Alaska, for which medical programme data were unavailable.

Note: - Detail may not add to totals due to rounding.

> The cumulative effect of markedly varying payment rates and eligibility level is that the Northern and North Central States are giving away about three times as many dollars as the Southern States relative to their populations of poor female-headed families with children. In the West, twice as many dollars per poor family are being spent as in the South. Put otherwise, about 37 per cent of poor female-headed families with related children under 18 were in the South in 1973, but only 17 per cent of AFDC funds were being spent there in 1974. By contrast, the North-east contained 22 per cent of such poor families but spent 34 per cent of such funds.

The average actual amount of monthly AFDC cash payment per recipient for the country as a whole was $66.79 in June 1955[1] or $801 annually. For a non-farm four-person family headed by a woman the annual sum amounted to $3,206 equivalent to 59 per cent of the corresponding poverty line income ($5,473). As between states the average monthly cash payment ranged from $14.41 or only 13 per cent of the poverty line income in Mississippi to $90.51 or 79 per cent of the poverty line income in Minnesota.[2]

It may be noted that though the average monthly payment per recipient was still low, the national average in real terms had increased by 10 per cent between 1960 and 1965 and by another 20 per cent between 1965 and 1970. However, there had been practically no further increase in real terms in the 1970s until the second half of 1975.[3] Thus, unlike the 1960s the expansion of public expenditure on AFDC in the 1970s was due mainly to the increase in the number of recipients.

(b) Weak response to the work incentive provisions

Before 1967 in most states the amount of benefit paid to the client under the AFDC programme was equal to the difference between the client's own income and the maximum payment standard of the needs standard depending on the state in question. If the family had no income, the benefit would equal the maximum payment standard or the needs standard. If the family head earned an income, the benefit would be reduced by that amount. There would be no increase in the family's total income. The marginal tax rate or benefit reduction rate was 100 per cent. This created a disincentive to work, for so long as its earnings were below the state's maximum

---

[1] US Department of Health, Education and Welfare, Social Security Bulletin, Vol. 39, No. 1, Jan. 1976, table M-33, p. 72. The average figure includes the children and one or both parents or one caretaker relative other than a parent in families in which the requirements of such adults were considered in determining the amount of assistance.

[2] ibid., p. 72.

[3] The trends in average AFDC cash payment in real terms described in this paragraph were based on the following December figures for monthly average per recipient in December 1974 dollars (except the 1975 figures): 49 in 1960; 54 in 1965; 65 in 1970; 66 in 1974; and 68 in September 1975. (Source: Economic Report of the President Transmitted to the Congress, January 1976, op. cit., p.97.)

payment or needs standards, generally work would not bring home any additional disposable income.[1]

In the face of a rapid growth of AFDC caseloads and of the public expenditure incurred, the Congress adopted in late 1967 new provisions know as the Work Incentive Programme (WIN) to give welfare parents financial incentives to work and "get off AFDC rolls". Effective in 1969, the new provisions contain, inter alia, the incentive formula of "$30 + 1/3 + work expenses". That is to say, for those who want to work "the first $30 of monthly earnings, plus one-third of remaining wages, plus work expenses, was to be ignored by welfare officials in computing benefits, even if this brought their total income - earnings plus welfare - above the State's needs standard."[2]

This incentive formula embodies the basic elements of a negative income tax. Besides encouraging the AFDC clients to work, it would also enable them to earn an income up to the neighbourhood of one and a half times the state's needs standard or maximum payment standard (the breakeven point) without losing completely the AFDC benefit even though the marginal tax rate or benefit reduction rate was high. In states where the needs or maximum payment standard was relatively high and reimbursement of work expenses liberal, this financial incentive could help AFDC mothers with good earnings potential move above the poverty line by the combined resources from earnings and AFDC benefits.[3]

---

[1] Several states had already introduced some kind of work incentive provisions before 1967.

[2] 93rd US Congress, 2nd Session: Joint Economic Committee: Income Security for Americans: Recommendations of the Public Welfare Study: Report of the Sub-committee on Fiscal Policy of the Joint Economic Committee, op. cit., p. 37.

[3] "In an attempt to restraint costs and caseloads, Congress withheld the work incentive bonus from non-welfare mothers already at work unless their total net income fell below their state's standard of need, the usual eligibility limit. Thus, if the state standard of need and payment standard were $3,500 for family on an annual basis, a woman earning $5,000 and having taxes and work expenses of $900 could not qualify for aid. However, her co-worker with the same wages and work expenses would be eligible for $1,305 in AFDC plus Medicaid if she had become a welfare recipient before taking the job. The new law prohibited the earnings exemption for persons who deliberately reduced their earnings or stopped working without good cause, but it was impossible to prevent some working women from taking advantage of the new rules by quitting work, applying for AFDC, and then resuming their job." (93rd Congress, 2nd Session: Joint Economic Committee: Income Security for Americans: Recommendations of the Public Welfare Study, op. cit., p. 38.)

Measures were also taken to provide training facilities for employable AFDC recipients. In June 1972 a more strict programme labelled WIN II was implemented requiring all employable AFDC recipients to register for training and placement services as a condition for receiving welfare benefits.

Methodologically it would be difficult to evaluate the response to the work incentive provisions in isolation from the influence of other factors. None the less, various studies have been made on this complex subject. These studies yield, among others, two seemingly contradictory findings:

1. AFDC recipients are highly motivated to work. One study showed that the commitment to work among welfare mothers was as strong as (or perhaps stronger than) that among non-welfare recipients.[1] A longitudinal study of recipients of AFDC programmes reached the same conclusion. It found that most of its sample welfare was not a "way of life" and that "the recipients wanted and requested job training which would lead them away from the brink of poverty, but were even more eager for a job."[2] These findings were further supported by the fact that "throughout its history the demand of volunteers for WIN work and training slots had exceeded the supply."[3]

2. The average proportion of AFDC mothers in employment was low. As of January 1973 only 16 per cent of AFDC mothers were employed.[4] Further, as revealed by periodic surveys of AFDC mothers, the percentage who were employed remained fairly stable at between 15 and 16 per cent from 1961 to 1973.[5] These data suggest a weak response to the work incentive provisions, and seem to contradict the high motivation to work among AFDC mothers shown in other studies cited above.

---

[1] Leonard Goodwin: Do the Poor Want to Work? (The Brookings Institution, Washington, D.C., 1972) cited in Michael C. Barth, George J. Carcagno and John L. Palmer: Towards an Effective Income Support System: Problems, Prospects and Choices (Institute for Research on Poverty, University of Wisconsin-Madison, 1974), p. 63.

[2] David S. Franklin: "A Longitudinal Study for WIN Dropouts: Programme and Policy Implications", University of Southern California, (April 1972), cited in Michael C. Barth, George J. Carcagno and John L. Palmer, op. cit., p. 63.

[3] Michael C. Barth, George J. Carcagno and John L. Palmer, op. cit., p. 63.

[4] 93rd US Congress, 2nd Session: Joint Economic Committee: Income Security For Americans: Recommendations of the Public Welfare Study, op. cit., p. 98. The figure was taken from Findings of the 1973 AFDC Study: Part I, Demographic and Program Characteristics, p. 58.

[5] Figures cited in Economic Report of the President Transmitted to the Congress, January 1976, op. cit., p. 99.

The contradiction was, however, more apparent than real for several reasons. First, the largest proportion of AFDC mothers were needed in the home to take care of their young children.[1] Even if they desired to work outside the home, they would not do so unless sufficient low-cost but adequate day-care services were available to meet their needs and their earnings high enough to make it worth while to pay the day-care expense. Second, for those who were available for jobs, jobs were not always available to them. This seemed particularly true during the 1974-75 recession when the female unemployment rates were high.[2]

Third, their level of education and skill being low, the jobs available to AFDC mothers usually paid low wages, and many of them were able to find only part-time jobs. The amount of net earnings after the deduction of work-related expenses and two-thirds of the earnings taxed away in relation to the AFDC benefits at zero earned income could be so small that they would find it not worth their work effort. If they did work, in many cases the income they earned would be too low to lift their families above the poverty line. The likelihood was that they had to depend continually on AFDC benefits as an essential income supplement. While more recent data were not available, the 1971 survey of AFDC mothers showed that those who worked earned an average of $223 per month[3] or $2,676 annually. This amount of earnings was equivalent to only 65 per cent of the poverty line for a non-farm family of four ($4,137) in 1971. Thus, regarding the AFDC population, as one study has defined succinctly, "the major problem is simply a lack of jobs paying adequate wages for the population in question".[4]

---

[1] "According to a 1971 survey by the Department of Health, Education and Welfare (HEW) out of 2.3 million AFDC mothers, 644,800 were seeking work, receiving training or awaiting training; 936,800 were needed full-time in the home; 478,000 were physically or mentally incapacitated or without marketable skills; and the remaining 286,100 or 12 per cent were not seeking work although presumably able to do so" (Henry J. Aaron: <u>Why is Welfare so Hard to Reform</u>? op. cit., p. 10).

[2] In March 1975, for example, female unemployment rates 16 years and over) were: for the widowed, divorced or separate, 8 per cent among Whites and 13 per cent among non-Whites; for single (never married), 10.8 among Whites and 22.3 per cent for non-Whites (US Department of Labour, Bureau of Labour Statistics: <u>Employment and Earnings</u>, Vol. 21, No. 10, Apr. 1975, p. 27).

[3] Figure cited in Henry J. Aaron: <u>Why is Welfare so Hard to Reform</u>? (The Brookings Institution, Washington, D.C., 1973, p. 10).

[4] Michael C. Barth, George J. Carcagno and John L. Palmer: <u>Toward an Effective Income Support System: Problems, Prospects and Choices</u>, with an Overview Paper by Irwin Garfinkel (Institute for Research on Poverty, University of Wisconsin-Madison, 1974), p. 103.

Fourth, though the national average rate of employment among AFDC mothers remains fairly stable despite the work incentive provisions, a comparative analysis of the situation in different states has shown a clear relationship between changes in the rate of employment among AFDC mothers and changes in the marginal tax rate or the benefit reduction rate. It was found that the highest rates of increase in the proportion of AFDC mothers employed between 1967 and 1973 took place among states that initiated the earnings exemption in 1969 and the greatest reduction in the employment of AFDC mothers occurred in states where financial incentive to work was reduced as a result of changing their payment structures to conform to the more restrictive national provision.[1] So, a lowering of benefit reduction rates did have a positive effect on AFDC employment. Another determining factor was the level of AFDC payments. Where the maximum payment standard was extremely low, say, between 30 per cent of the poverty line, many of the AFDC mothers would probably have no choice but to enter the labour market working for very low wages. Low earnings combined with low AFDC benefit would bring them some little additional income that they needed so badly, and the latter amount would depend partly on the benefit reduction rate.[2]

(c) Automatic eligibility for in-kind transfers

With the rapid expansion of in-kind assistance programmes and automatic eligibility of recipients of cash assistance for benefits under these programmes, the low level of AFDC benefits noted earlier had been supplemented increasingly by in-kind benefits. Most important among these were food stamps and medicaid; others included, inter alia, free school lunch and public or subsidised housing. Table II.7 gives an approximate quantitative indication of the difference that food stamp bonus and medicaid made to the amount of public assistance income received by a penniless mother with three children in 1974. Three significant facts emerged from the table:

---

[1] 93rd US Congress, 2nd Session, Joint Committee Print: Income Security for Americans: Recommendations of the Public Welfare Study: Report of the Sub-committee on Fiscal Policy of the Joint Economic Committee, op. cit., p. 101.

[2] A multiple regression analysis made by Irwin Garfinkel and Larry L. Orr yields certain estimates of the effects of cash payment levels and benefit loss rates on employment rates of AFDC mothers. "Their estimates suggest that considerable liberalisation of earnings deductions and benefit loss rates and reduction of payment levels might more than double AFDC mothers' employment rates. Even so, half or more would not be induced to work or could or would not work continuously, according to their estimates." (ibid., p. 101.)

1. The combined support levels (maximum AFDC payment plus allowable food stamp bonus) were indeed considerably higher than the maximum AFDC payment levels alone. Twelve states with their maximum AFDC payment levels below 40 per cent of the povery line all moved up to or above that ratio with the addition of food stamp bonus. These states covered 23 per cent of the total number of AFDC families (3.2 million) in February 1974.

2. Even with the addition of food stamp bonus only in three states did the combined support level exceed the poverty line covering about 12 per cent of the total AFDC families. Fifty per cent of AFDC families lived in states with a combined support level between 80 and 99 per cent of the poverty line. This was an improvement compared to 29 per cent falling within this range when maximum AFDC payment alone was counted. However, there were still 14 states with a combined support level between 40 and 70 per cent of the poverty line and these states covered about 26 per cent of the total AFDC families.

3. Medicaid doubtless filled a vital need of AFDC mothers. But as the table indicates, the amount of medicaid payment for an AFDC family appeared to vary directly with the AFDC maximum support level.

Recent information on the extent of participation of AFDC families in different in-kind assistance programmes is not readily available. An earlier 1973 survey showed that 99 per cent of AFDC families received medicaid; 59.7 per cent, food stamps; 8.9 per cent, food distribution (surplus commodities); and 13.6 per cent, public housing.[1] The percentage of AFDC families receiving food is likely to have increased in 1974 and 1975 with the increase in the total number of food stamp participants during these years.

The automatic elibibility of AFDC families for in-kind benefits contributed greatly to raising their low levels of living set by low levels of AFDC benefits in a great many states. However, multiple benefits have built disincentives to work effort into its structure. Although the actual impact of disincentive effects is not yet clearly known, these effects can be identified as follows:[2]

---

[1] Cited in 93rd US Congress, 2nd Session: Joint Committee Print: Income Security for Americans: Recommendations of the Public Welfare Study, op. cit., p. 62.

[2] For a detailed study of the effects of multiple benefits, see 92nd US Congress, 2nd Session, Joint Committee Print: Studies in Public Welfare: Paper No. 1: Public Income Transfer Programmes: the Incidence of Multiple Benefits and the Issues Raised by their Recipient, A study prepared for the use of the Sub-committee on Fiscal Policy of the Joint Economic Committee by James R. Storey. (US Government Printing Office, 1972.)

1. The effect of cumulative tax rate or benefit reduction rate. Like AFDC programmes, several of the in-kind assistance programmes reduced benefits with increases in income. Food stamps and public housing were programmes of this type. As an AFDC family's income rises, the family would have to pay a higher price for the same food stamp allotment and an increased rent for public housing, in addition to a reduction in the AFDC benefit. Even if considered separately each programme's benefit reduction rate was low; in combination such programmes could result in rather high reduction rates. It has been shown that if the three programmes mentioned above operated in combination, a marginal benefit reduction rate of 85 cents for each additional dollar earnings would result.[1] In other words, each additional dollar earned could add only 15 cents to the total disposable income.

2. The "income notch" effect. Several other in-kind programmes provided constant levels of benefits to AFDC families, as to other public assistance recipients, regardless of income so long as the families retained eligibility for AFDC benefits. But as soon as the family's income exceeds the income standard used to define eligibility for the AFDC programme, the loss of AFDC eligibility would be accompanied by a sudden complete loss of benefits from all these programmes. "To illustrate, family earnings might increase by only $100, but programme rules could cause a loss of benefits in excess of $300. In this example, total family income would decline by over $200, or more than twice the increase in earned income."[2] An income notch thus occurred.

---

[1] "For example, when an AFDC recipient earns extra dollars, she can expect a net gain of at least 33 cents per dollar. But if she receives other benefits, they, too, will be cut; the food stamp programme, taking note of her 33 cent per dollar net cash gain, will raise stamp prices 10 cents per extra dollar (30 per cent of the extra net income); public housing will raise rent by 8 cents per extra dollar. Thus the cumulative take-back rate could climb to 85 cents. It does not seem reasonable to expect persons to work for a net gain of only 15 per cent per extra dollar, especially at possibly unpleasant work." (93rd US Congress, 2nd Session: Joint Committee Print: Income Security for Americans: Recommendations on the Public Welfare Policy, op. cit., p. 77.)

[2] 92nd US Congress, 2nd Session: Joint Committee Print: Studies in Public Welfare: Paper No. 1, Public Income Transfer Programmes: The Incidence of Multiple Benefits and the Issues Raised by their Receipt prepared by James R. Storey, op. cit., pp. 9-10.

Medicaid, food distribution (surplus commodities) and school lunch programmes were programmes of this second type. In the case of medicaid, with the large amounts of benefits involved the income notch effect could be particularly serious. For many AFDC families, it would be to their advantage to refrain from further increasing their earned income if only to retain their eligibility for medicaid.

Socially, AFDC could be an inducement to family splitting. Since AFDC was not available to families with dependent children headed by an able-bodied, employed father and since the wages earned by many employed fathers were low and indeed lower than the combined AFDC-support level (maximum AFDC cash payment plus in-kind benefits) there were financial incentives for low-wage male family heads to leave home in order to enable their families to qualify for AFDC and other benefits.[1]

As noted previously, unemployed fathers were eligible for AFDC after the 1967 social security amendments under the AFDC-UF programme if they satisfied other conditions of AFDC eligibility as well as special conditions for unemployed fathers. These conditions included the stipulation that "the father must have been unemployed for at least 30 days, have had sufficient work experience to satisfy a minimum requirement, be seeking and available for work, and be unemployed or working less than 100 hours per month".[2] The provision of "working less than 100 hours per month" created an "income notch" discouraging full-time work for low-wage workers. For the earnings of a low-wage full-time worker could be appreciably lower than total income

---

[1] The Sub-committee on Fiscal Policy of the Joint Economic Committee of the US Congress gave the following illustrative example based on data prevailing in North Dakota in July 1974:

Working father at home Two-parent family, three children		Father absent Broken family, mother and three children	
Net earnings[(a)] $2 per hour job	$278	Maximum AFDC benefit	$300
Food stamp bonus (July 1974)	100	Food stamp bonus	67
Medicaid	-	Medicaid	70
	$378		$437

(a) Assume $35 in bus fare and other expenses plus $20 payroll tax. If father "deserted", family could pool $437 in welfare benefits and $278 in net wages for total of $715". (93rd Congress, 2nd Session: Joint Economic Committee: Income Security for Americans: Recommendations of the Public Welfare Study: Report of the Sub-committee on Fiscal Policy of the Joint Economic Committee, op. cit. p. 79.)

[2] Economic Report of the President Transmitted to the Congress, January, 1976, op. cit., p. 100.

from part-time work plus welfare benefits.[1] In 1975 AFDC-UF programmes operated in 26 states. About 113,000 families received AFDC-UF benefits in July 1975, and the average cash benefit per family was $311 (equivalent to 68 per cent of the poverty line for a non-farm family of four), in addition to eligibility for food stamps and medicaid benefits.[2]

General assistance

General assistance is treated in this study as a major component of public transfer payments because of its potential importance. It was practically the only type of public cash assistance available for the vast numbers of needy persons not entitled to the categorical programmes. Programmes under general assistance were financed and administered entirely by state and local governments without federal participation. The main features of such programmes are briefly described below.

Resources. The over-all size of general assistance programmes operating in the country, as stressed earlier, was quite small in relation to the need for such assistance. In 1975 the total amount of cash payment under general assistance was 1.1 billion current dollars compared to 9.2 billion under AFDC, and in December 1975 the number of general assistance recipients totalled about 1 million compared to a total of 11.4 million recipients of AFDC benefits.[3] Thus, the size of general assistance was roughly only one-tenth of that of AFDC.

Uneven distribution. Furthermore, the distribution of general assistance payments was highly uneven between different areas. As one study has shown, in January 1974, 55 per cent of the total amount of general assistance payments made by 44 states and the District of Columbia were concentrated in 17 large cities and counties.[4] The inter-state variation in average monthly

---

[1] In discussing this question, the Sub-committee on Fiscal Policy of the Joint Economic Committee gave the following example: "A man with a wife and three children who took a full-time job at $1.60 an hour in July 1972 received an after-tax income of $3,034, but lost AFDC-UF benefits of $3,840 in San Francisco or $3,588 in Portland, Oregan". (93rd US Congress, 2nd Session: Joint Committee Print: Income Security for Americans: Recommendations of the Public Welfare Study: Report of the Sub-committee on Fiscal Policy of the Joint Economic Committee, op. cit., p. 40.)

[2] Economic Report of the President Transmitted to the Congress, January 1976, op. cit., p. 100.

[3] US Department of Health, Education and Welfare: Social Security Bulletin, Vol. 29, No. 11, Nov. 1976, table M-32 and table M-33, pp. 75-76.

[4] 93rd US Congress, 2nd Session: Joint Economic Committee: Income Security for Americans: Recommendations of the Public Welfare Study, op. cit. p. 43.

general assistance per recipient was even greater than that under AFDC programmes. In June 1975 it ranged from $10.75 in Oklahoma and $12.20 in Mississippi to $117.57 in Pennsylvania and $125.35 in Michigan[1] or from 9 per cent of the poverty line for a non-farm family of four at the bottom to 109 per cent at the top. As a national average the monthly general assistance payment per recipient in June 1975 was $98.76 in June 1955 which was about 48 per cent higher than the corresponding figure for AFDC.[2] The general assistance recipients consisted chiefly of the able-bodied men and their families, childless couples and single individuals. "Frequently, General Assistance is limited to short-term or emergency assistance, but in some states - New York, for example, - continuing aid is provided to the working poor".[3]

Virtual absence of work incentive provision. Unlike AFDC and many other types of public assistance, general assistance programmes, as a rule, provided little or no financial work incentives. The marginal tax rate or benefit reduction rate was usually 100 per cent. So long as the family's earnings were below the general assistance benefit level any increase in earnings would cause a reduction of benefits to the same. Some localities, however, made allowance for certain work expenses in computing benefits. One reason for not introducing a lower rate of benefit reduction was that this would raise the cost of the programmes, and most state and local governments were unable to afford it.

Medicaid

Medicaid, together with medicare for the aged, was enacted as part of the 1965 social security amendments under title XIX. The main purpose of the medicaid programme was to enable states, at their option, to provide more adequate medical assistance to persons covered by the four federal categorical assistance programmes (AFDC and aid to the aged, blind and disabled) by expansion of federal financial support. As explained earlier, in addition to the recipients of benefits under these specific programmes, states could also secure federal support for medical assistance to persons who are in the same eligible categories and whose incomes were not more than one-third above the needs standard in that state for cash assistance (the "medically needy" or "medically indigent"). States might also choose to provide

---

[1] US Department of Health, Education and Welfare: Social Security Bulletin, Vol. 39, No. 1, Jan. 1976, table M-33, p. 72.

[2] ibid., p. 72.

[3] Michael C. Barth, George J. Carcagno and John L. Palmer, Toward an Effective Income Support System: Problems, Prospects and Choices, op. cit., p. 24.

medicaid to persons who were "medically needy" but not "categorically related". For such cases federal funds were available for administrative costs only.[1]

Since its inception in 1966 medicaid has grown into the largest of the federal-state jointly financed public assistance programmes. The total amount of medicaid payments increased from $1.2 billion in 1966 to $5.5 billion in 1970 and to about $14 billion in 1975.[2] Deflated by the price index for medical care,[3] the amount in real terms spent in 1975 was 6.4 times the amount incurred in 1965. The number of persons receiving medicaid benefits increased from 15.5 million in 1970 to 23 million in 1974[4] and was expected to rise to 26 million in 1976.[5]

The enormous size of the medicaid programme and its rapid rate of growth should have generated a considerable impact on poverty alleviation. For several reasons, the actual impact is likely to have been less, perhaps much less, than its over-all size would suggest.

---

[1] 93rd US Congress, 1st Session, Joint Economic Committee, Sub-committee on Fiscal Policy: Studies on Public Welfare: Paper No. 8: Income-Tested Social Benefits in New York: Adequacy, Incentives and Equity, prepared by Blanche Bernstein with Anne N. Shkuda and Eveline M. Burns, 8 July 1973. (US Government Printing Office, Washington, 1973), p. 53.

[2] These figures refer to total medical vendor payments made under federally-aided medical assistance programmes, taken from US Department of Health, Education and Welfare: Social Security Bulletin, Vol. 39. No. 11, Nov. 1976, table M-35, p. 78. These figures are higher than the corresponding figures for medicaid payments given in Alfred M. Skolnik and Sophie R. Dales: "Social Welfare Expenditures, 1950-75", in Social Security Bulletin, Vol. 39, No. 1, Jan. 1976, p. 6. The difference was probably due largely to the fact that the former refer to calendar year and the latter to fiscal year.

[3] The price indexes for medical care (1967=100) for 1966, 1970 and 1975 are, respectively, 93.4, 120.6 and 168.6, taken from Social Security Bulletin, Vol. 39, No. 11, Nov. 1976, p. 83.

[4] Economic Report of the President Transmitted to the Congress, January 1976, op. cit., p. 123.

[5] Executive Office of the President, Office of Management and Budget: The United States Budget in Brief: Fiscal Year 1976 (Washington, D.C.), p. 35.

First, medicaid was primarily a specific programme. Despite its rapid growth in expenditure, those who were poor but not eligible for the four categorical programmes benefited relatively little from medicaid. As shown in table II.8, of a total of $809.3 million of medicaid payments made in August 1973 only 7.5 per cent went for persons other than "categorical eligibles". These persons were "medically needy" but not "categorically related". And it is important to remember that by definition a "medically needy" or "medically indigent" family already had an income one-third above the needs standard in that state.[1] Thus, it seemed that large numbers of persons - persons in intact families headed by a working father or an unemployed father not on AFDC-UF, non-aged childless couples and single individuals - could not count on medicaid to keep them from falling further below the poverty line because of heavy medical expenses they might incur.

Second, since states had power to determine eligibility limits, the proportion of persons entitled to medicaid varied greatly in different states. As of 1974, 25 states and district of Columbia extended the medicaid programme to cover the "medically indigents"; in 24 states, including the majority of southern states, the medicaid programme was restricted to recipients of federally financed cash assistance.[2] In 1973, 18 states extended medicaid to cover children under 21 in intact families but not covering parents.[3]

---

[1] On this definition of a "medically needy" or "medically indigent" Professor Theodore E. Marmor made the following observations: "Odd effects are produced by this definition of medical indigence wherein medical care costs reduce incomes to below the state-set income level for basic maintenance needs. This "protected" income level may not exceed 133 per cent of the maximum amount payable to AFDC recipient families of comparable size. It means that all poor people who are not aged, blind, disabled, or with children under 21 cannot be treated as medical indigents. It is another anomaly highlighted by the rediscovery of the working poor in connection with recent welfare reform efforts. Equally poor families which are not in the appropriate demographic categories are thus not equally eligible for even the medically indigent programme under medicaid." Theodore R. Marmor: "Public Medical Programmes and Cash Assistance: The Problems of Programme Integration", in 93rd US Congress, 1st Session: Joint Economic Committee: Studies in Public Welfare: Paper No. 7: Issues in the Co-ordination of Public Welfare Programmes: A volume of studies prepared for the use of the Sub-committee on Fiscal Policy of the Joint Economic Committee, 2 July 1973 (US Government Printing Office, Washington, 1973), pp. 89-90.

[2] 93rd US Congress, 2nd Session, Joint Economic Committee: Income Security for Americans: Recommendations of the Public Welfare Study: Report of the Sub-committee on Fiscal Policy of the Joint Economic Committee, op. cit., p. 66.

[3] Irene Cox: "Treatment of Families Under Income Transfer Programmes", in 93rd US Congress, 1st Session, Joint Economic Committee: Studies in Public Welfare: Paper No. 12 (Part II): The Family, Poverty and Welfare Programmes: Household Patterns and Government Policies: A volume of studies prepared for the use of the Sub-committee on Fiscal Policy of the Joint Economic Committee, 3 Dec. 1973 (US Government Printing Office, Washington, 1973), p. 192.

Table II.8

Medicaid Payments by Eligibility Groups, August 1973
(in millions of dollars)

Base of eligibility	Total vendor payments	Per cent of total	Cash welfare status of beneficiaries: Beneficiaries also getting cash welfare	Per cent of total	Medically needy categories	Per cent of total
Aged 65 and over	$ 283.8	35.1	$ 84.0	19.2	$ 199.8	53.6
Blindness	6.9	0.8	4.9	1.1	2.0	0.5
Permanent and total disability	187.5	23.2	125.9	28.9	61.6	16.5
Families with dependent children	270.1	33.4	221.5	50.8	48.6	13.0
Others	61.0	7.5	-	-	61.0	16.4
Total	809.3	100.0	436.3	100.0	373.0	100.0

Source: US Department of Health, Education and Welfare, National Center for Social Statistics: "Medical Assistance (medicaid) Financed under Title XIX of the Social Security Amendment, August 1973" reproduced in the 93rd, 2nd Session, Joint Economic Committee: Income Security For Americans: Recommendations of the Public Welfare Study: Report of the Sub-committee on Fiscal Policy of the Joint Economic Committee, 5 Dec. 1974 (US Government Printing Office, Washington, 1974), p. 66.

Third, states also had much flexibility in selecting and setting limits to, medical services to be covered by medicaid thereby determining its benefit coverage. Moreover, availability for medical care varied in different states. These factors resulted in a wide inter-state variation in medicaid benefits per eligible family or recipient. Medicaid benefits took the form of payments to providers of medical care services; the reimbursable services were specified by the states. Generally, the benefits paid in poor states (especially in the south) were much lower than in affluent states. As illustrated in table II.7, there was a positive association between the amount of medicaid payment per AFDC family and the maximum AFDC payment level. In fiscal 1972 the estimated average medicaid payments for families eligible for AFDC ranged from $50 per family in Mississippi to

$1,150 per family in California.[1] Like AFDC, the medicaid expenditure was marked by a highly uneven distribution between states. In February 1973 three affluent states - New York, California and Michigan - accounted for almost 42 per cent of all medicaid expenditures.[2] With the object of encouraging poor states to increase their expenditures on medicaid and of eliminating regional disparity, a special formula for federal reimbursement to the state for the medicaid programme based on per capita income of each state was adopted. For the high-income states the 1965 social security amendments allowed 50 per cent federal matching, but in those states with the lowest per capita incomes, federal grants could reach as high as 83 per cent. One earlier study of its effect in 1968 showed that after two-and-a-half years of medicaid the differences in medicaid payments between wealthy states and poor states had become more, not less, pronounced.[3] Besides, there were other variations in benefits among those covered by medicaid. It observed that payments for Whites were considerably higher per recipient than for Blacks and there was a striking difference in medicaid benefits per recipient between rural and urban residents.[4]

In brief, while by virtue of its size the over-all impact of medicaid on poverty might be substantial, the distribution of its impact appears to have been highly uneven between poverty populations of different demographic characteristics, between rich and poor states, and between recipients of different races and at different places of residence. As a result of uneven distribution of its benefits, the total number of persons lifted above the poverty line by the medicaid programme was probably appreciably smaller than the programme would otherwise have been capable of.

It may also be recalled that medicaid had a severe "notch" effect which created a strong disincentive to work effort not only for AFDC recipients but equally for other medicaid recipients.

---

[1] Michael C. Barth, George J. Carcagno and John L. Palmer: Toward an Effective Income Support System: Problems, Prospects and Choices, op. cit., p. 21.

[2] ibid., p. 21.

[3] See Bruce C. Stuart: "The Impact of Medicaid on Interstate Income Differentials", in Kenneth E. Boulding and Martin Pfaff: Redistribution to the Rich and the Poor (Wadsworth Publishing Company, Belmont, California, 1972), p. 167.

[4] Karen Davis: "National Health Insurance", in Barry M. Blechman, Edward Gramlich and Robert W. Hartman: Setting National Priorities: The 1975 Budget (The Brookings Institution, Washington, D.C., 1974), p. 211.

Food stamps

The Federal Government had a variety of food assistance programmes for improving the diet of low-income households.[1] The food stamp programme was by far the largest. It was first enacted in 1964 as an alternative to the direct distribution of surplus food commodities. Started on a modest scale, the programme has since undergone several legislative amendments. The 1973 amendments mandated nationwide expansion of the food stamp programme by 30 June 1974. The programme was financed wholly from federal funds and administered by the Department of Agriculture through local and state welfare offices.

Unlike medicaid and other federal participating public assistance programmes, the food stamp programme was non-specific and universal in coverage and with uniform eligibility requirements and uniform benefit schedules maintained throughout the country.

Under the food stamp programme a low-income household could buy from the local welfare agency a monthly food stamp allotment at a cost varying with its monthly net income. The household could purchase most food items at face value with these coupons in grocery stores. Food stamps were redeemed through normal banking procedures.

The amount of monthly food stamp allotment a household could buy depended on household size and was based on the Department of Agriculture's Thrifty Food Plan for the corresponding household size. The face value of the food stamp allotment was the market cost of the foods that made up the food plan adjusted twice a year for changes in the price of these foods.

The difference between the face value of the food stamp allotment and the purchse price of the food stamp allotment was the food stamp "bonus" or federal food subsidy.

As regards eligibility requirements, households in which all members were receiving public assistance were automatically eligible for food stamps. For all other households the programme set maximum allowable monthly net income standards[2] or income cut-off lines for households of different size. Like food stamp allotment, the income cut-off lines were adjusted twice a year for changes in the cost of living. The 125 per cent of the poverty

---

[1] In addition to food stamps and distribution of surplus food commodities, other federal food programmes comprised national school lunch programme, school breakfast programme, special pre-school food service programme, special milk programme and special summer service programme.

[2] Net income was gross money income (including, inter alia, cash public assistance) less a number of deductions of household expenses listed in the food stamp regulations. Each household was allowed up to $1,500 in liquid and certain non-liquid assets. The asset limitation was $3,000 for households with a member aged 60 or more. Work registration was required for eligibility of food stamps.

line was regarded as a rough minimum measure of income eligibility for food stamps.[1] As of December 1974 the income cut-off line ranged from $210 a month for a single-person household, $510 for a 4-person household to $870 for an 8-person household.[2]

Below the income cut-off lines the purchase price of monthly food stamp allotment, allowing for some variation, rose about $3 for each $10 increase in net income or a 30 per cent benefit reduction rate after a $30 net income. For example, in December 1974 the face value of monthly food stamp allotment for a family of four persons was $150. The purchase price of the stamp allotment at this value was nil for a four-person family with a monthly net income below $30, rose to $10 at a net income between $50-$60, $25 at a net income between $100-$110, $95 at a net income between $330-$360, up to $126 at a net income between $450-$480.[3] As soon as the household monthly net income reached the cut-off line of $480, the purchase price would equal the face value of the stamp allotment. The federal food subsidy in this example thus started with $150, then with the given successive increases in net income diminished from $140 to $125, $55, $24 and finally to zero.

Earlier studies of the relationship of food stamp bonus and other sources of income of low-income households participating in the food stamp programme revealed significant findings:

1. A national sample survey of food stamp households conducted in November 1973 showed that the average income of food stamp households surveyed was $364 per month or $4,358 annually; that earnings from wages and other private sources accounted for only 20 per cent of this amount of income and the remaining 80 per cent was public transfer income either in cash or in kind (45 per cent in cash and 35 per cent in kind); that the four main sources of federal transfer income were (i) AFDC, $72, (ii) medicaid, $59, (iii) social security, $54 and (iv) food stamp bonus, $49; that female-headed households accounted for 70 per cent of Black and 60 per cent of White food stamp receiving households; that some 70 per cent of household heads were not in the labour force (51 per cent unemployed and not seeking work, and 18 per cent retired) and only 13 per cent were employed full-time.[4]

---

[1] 93rd US Congress, Joint Economic Committee: Studies in Public Welfare: Paper No. 17, <u>National Survey of Food Stamp and Food Distribution Programme Recipients: A Summary of Findings on Income Sources and Amounts and Incidence of Multiple Benefits</u>: A study prepared for the use of the Sub-committee on Fiscal Policy of the Joint Economic Committee; 31 Dec. 1974 (US Government Printing Office, Washington 1974), p. 18.

[2] ibid., p. 21.

[3] ibid., p. 21.

[4] ibid., pp. 8-9 and p. 15.

2. In contrast to medicaid, a clear inverse relation was found between food stamp bonus and AFDC payments. As one study relating to a four-person family with no earned income has shown, the five states with lowest maximum payment for basic needs had an average maximum AFDC payment in 1973 of $102 per month, but the average monthly food stamp bonus was high at $121. Thus, the total family resources were $223. Conversely, the five states with highest maximum payment for basic needs had an average maximum AFDC payment of $350, but food stamp bonuses were lower at $49. Thus, the total family resources were $399.[1] Consequently, the operation of the food stamp programme tended to reduce inter-state differences in the incomes of the poverty population. It was observed, however, that "even when food stamp bonuses are counted as regular income, mothers with children who receive aid only from AFDC and food stamps remain well below the poverty line, especially in low-paying states."[2]

The food stamp programme was expanding rapidly during the first half of the 1970s, especially since the 1973 amendment. The number of participants increased from 4.3 million in fiscal 1970 to 12.9 million in fiscal 1974 and 17.1 million in fiscal 1975.[3] The federal cost of the programme rose correspondingly from $550 million to $2.7 billion and to $4.4 billion in fiscal 1975[4] or nearly tripled in real terms[5] over the five-year period. One factor contributing to its expansion was the shift from food commodities distribution. Another factor was high inflation and high unemployment during the 1974-75 recession. Since most other public assistance programmes were specific, many low-income households suffering from adverse effects of inflation and unemployment turned to food stamps for financial assistance. With the programme mandated to be nationwide in coverage the number of population eligible for food stamps was in fact far greater than the number of participants. "Unpublished studies indicate that at some time during the year ending 1 July 1977 a total of 60 million Americans might be eligible for food stamps on an income basis (compared with an expected peak of 50 million eligible at some time in the fiscal year 1974)".[6]

---

[1] Barry M. Blechman, Edward M. Gramlich and Robert W. Hartman: Setting National Priorities: The 1975 Budget (The Brookings Institution, Washington, D.C., 1974), p. 179.

[2] ibid., p. 179.

[3] Economic Report of the President Transmitted to the Congress, January 1976, op. cit., p. 102.

[4] ibid., p. 102.

[5] Deflated by the price index for food (1967=100) which was 114.9 in 1970, 161.7 in 1974 and 175.4 in 1975.

[6] 93rd US Congress, 2nd Session, Joint Economic Committee: Income Security for Americans: Recommendations of the Public Welfare Study, op. cit., p. 45.

As an instrument for poverty alleviation, the food stamp programme has, however, a number of limitations. First, many poor households may not have enough cash to purchase the monthly food stamps allotment for the whole month in advance. Secondly, the real value of food stamps to a very poor household could be much less than the cost to the Government when food stamps formed a predominant portion of its total real income and the household was in dire need of other essentials. Data for the early 1970s showed that in Mississippi a family headed by a welfare mother of three children with no other outside income would have to spend 76 per cent of its combined AFDC maximum cash benefits plus food stamp income on food in Mississippi; in Alabama, 69 per cent; in Ohio, 50 per cent.[1] And there were reports of Black market sales of food stamps at a significant discount.[2] Thirdly, the food stamp programme was considered by some writers as a demeaning programme "that needlessly makes its beneficiaries reveal their dependent status to grocery clerks and casual observers.[3] Moreover, for the food stamp programme, its nutritional goals are "so diluted by the broader population served and the total reliance on consumer choice that it relates much more to the purposes of general income maintenance and to programmes such as aid to families with dependent children (AFDC) and supplemental security income (SSI) than to a nutrition programme such as WIC."[4] For these various reasons there is a case for replacing the food stamp bonus by cash assistance with no restrictions imposed on the freedom of choice of the poor.[5]

Public employment

For poverty alleviation public employment schemes are of several distinctive types. One type is the provision of public jobs to employable welfare recipients so as to enable them to earn an income from work instead of living totally on public assistance. The work incentive formulas built into the determination of public assistance benefits and work registration

---

[1] 93rd US Congress, 2nd Session, Joint Economic Committee: Income Security for Americans: Recommendations of the Public Welfare Study, op. cit., pp. 137-138. According to the data cited, for a welfare mother of three children the maximum monthly AFDC cash payment was $260 and the monthly food stamp allotment was worth $150 for $13.

[2] ibid., p. 138.

[3] Gilbert Y. Steiner: The State of Welfare (The Brookings Institution, Washington, D.C., 1971), p. 319; and also p. 236.

[4] James R. Storey: "Social Policy Roles of Food Assistance Programme", American Journal of Agricultural Economics, Vol. XXXXII No. 10, Dec. 1976, p. 1011. WIC refers to the special nutrition programmes for women, infants and children who have special nutritional needs.

[5] Gilbert Y. Steiner, op. cit., p. 319.

as part of eligibility requirements were all designed to induce the recipients to take up gainful employment. Since the majority of welfare recipients had a low level of skills, training programmes were instituted (e.g. the Work Incentive (WIN) Programme) to help them to acquire more productive skills and thereby enhance their earning capacity. However, even with their newly acquired skills, jobs might not be available to them, or at least not in sufficient numbers, for various reasons. Under such conditions, the Government would need to provide them with public jobs at adequate wages. In the United States it seems that public action in helping welfare recipients toward self-sufficiency had gone as far as training and manpower services. There were practically no public employment programmes designed specifically for welfare recipients as a means of overcoming chronic poverty.

In the United States as in many other countries, public employment was taken as a means of reducing unemployment during economic recessions. In the post-war era the first public employment programme (PEP) as a counter-cyclical measure was established by the Emergency Act of 1971. The programme was to provide "transitional" jobs when the unemployment rate was about 6 per cent. It was financed by the Federal Government but administered by states and local governments. In fiscal 1973, an estimated 150,000 man-years were funded by the PEP programme.[1]

The Emergency Employment Act was replaced in 1973 by the Comprehensive Employment and Training Act (CETA) which became operative in 1974. This new Act, besides providing funds for manpower training, also provided funds for public employment to states and localities as prime sponsors under its four titles. The estimated outlays on various parts of CETA for fiscal year 1975 totalled about $2.8 billion. It was expected that the number of public service jobs under CETA would increase from approximately 85,000 in fiscal year 1974 to 170,000 during 1975 and 1976.

As a supplement to CETA a Temporary Employment Assistance (TEA) Programme was created by the Emergency Job and Unemployment Assistance Act adopted by the Congress in December 1974. Under this temporary programme about 110,000 public service jobs would be created.

Thus, in fiscal 1975 the public employment programmes under CETA together with the Temporary Employment Assistance Programme would provide up to 280,000 public service jobs. This number was about 3.5 per cent of the total number of unemployed (about 8 million) in October 1975. The impact of public service employment on the over-all unemployment situation was therefore quite small.

---

[1] Material from this and the following paragraph on public service employment was drawn from the Economic Report of the President Transmitted to the Congress, February 1975 (US Government Printing Office, Washington, 1975), pp. 124-127.

Some further observations may be made. First, the gross figure of 280,000 jobs refers to jobs funded by federal money under these temporary and emergency employment programmes. The net additions to employment would be even smaller owing to the "displacement effect" - i.e. the effect of substituting federal for state and local funds on jobs that would have been provided in any case. According to past experience, the displacement effect would increase as time passes. Second, for public service jobs created under CETA, compensation and administration costs per man-year in fiscal 1975 was estimated at about $9,000. Although the average wage should be lower than this figure, it was probably much higher than the poverty line for a four-person non-farm family. Third, earlier experience of the public employment programme (PEP) showed that "participants were more likely than the average unemployed person to be veterans, male and well educated (75 per cent had graduated from high school)".[1] In the absence of relevant data it is difficult to ascertain how far the experience with the 1975 public employment programmes differed from this earlier experience. Nevertheless, it seems highly probable that the low-wage unskilled unemployed benefited little from the small size of public service employment.

The impact of income maintenance programmes on poverty reduction

The present section proceeds to discuss the extent to which the income maintenance programmes described above have reduced poverty in the country. So far as the over-all impact of public cash transfers on the level of poverty is concerned, some analysis has already been made in Chapter 1. Here, emphasis is more on the effects of different programmes and on different groups of the poverty population.

By the classification used in this chapter, public income maintenance expenditure, with its rapid growth in the 1970s, reached $188 billion in 1975 or 2.5 times the 1965 level in real terms.[2] With respect to its impact on poverty reduction, two features of the expenditure deserve special notice.

First, a substantial part of the income maintenance expenditure went to persons living above the poverty line. The proportion thus distributed varied greatly among different programmes. According to the estimates by Plotnick and Skidmore,

---

[1] Economic Report of the President Transmitted to the Congress, February 1975, op. cit., p. 124.

[2] Deflators based on implicit price deflator for personal consumption expenditures prepared for the national income accounts by the Department of Commerce: 1975 = 100, 1965 = 63.6. (Source: Alfred M. Skolnik and Sophie R. Dales: "Social Welfare Expenditures: 1970-75", loc. cit., p. 10.

in 1972, pre-transfer poor families (including unrelated individuals as single-person families) received 53 per cent of public cash transfers,[1] 85 per cent of federal payments on food stamp bonus, 55 per cent of benefits from other nutrition programmes, 75 per cent of medicaid payment, 48 per cent of medicare payment, and 74 per cent of public expenditure on public housing.[2] Using a different classification of income maintenance programmes, the Congressional Budget Office study referred to earlier, estimated that in fiscal year 1976, the poorest 20 per cent of families before public transfers received 32 per cent of the total benefits under cash social insurance programmes, 61 per cent of cash assistance benefits, 48 per cent of in-kind transfers under group I and 53 per cent of in-kind transfers under group II (medicare and medicaid benefits), as shown in table II.9. It may be added that a fraction of the pre-transfer poor families fell in the second lowest income quintile. It may also be stressed that many, but not all, of the non-poor who benefited from public income maintenance expenditures had pre-transfer incomes only moderately above the official poverty line. They belonged in the category of "near-poor". By a higher poverty standard they might well be counted as poor.

Second, as indicated previously, along with the expansion of income maintenance expenditures an increasing proportion consisted of in-kind transfers, though cash transfers continued to assume by far the larger part. By the classification used in this chapter, between 1965 and 1975 total in-kind transfers increased from $5.7 billion to $52.4 billion or by 4.7 times in real terms, whereas total cash transfers increased from $37 billion to $139 billion or by 1.4 times in real terms. The proportion of total income maintenance expenditure allotted to in-kind transfer programmes rose from 13 per cent to 27 per cent and that allotted to cash transfer programmes fell from 87 per cent to 73 per cent. The growing importance of in-kind transfers would, therefore, make it necessary to take carefully into account the effects of in-kind transfers in assessing the impact of public income maintenance programmes. Estimation of effects of in-kind transfers on poverty reduction, however, presents methodological problems of its own. For instance, it has been observed that "empirical evidence for 1974 and several earlier years indicated that, if food stamps were included as income and if the poverty thresholds were not changed, about 5 to 15 per cent of the poor (depending on the method of evaluation used) would no longer be counted as poor."[3]

---

[1] Among different public cash transfer programmes the percentage of public expenditure spent on pre-transfer poor varies as follows: social security and railroad benefits, 58; public employee retirement, 38; unemployment insurance, 21; workmen's compensation, 33; public assistance, 87; veteran's benefits, 43; and temporary disability, 21.

[2] Robert D. Plotnick and Felicity Skidmore, op. cit., p. 56.

[3] Department of Health, Education and Welfare: The Measure of Poverty, A Report to the Congress as Mandated by the Education Amendment of 1974 (Washington, D.C., 1976): Executive Summary, reproduced in Department of Health, Education and Welfare: Social Security Bulletin, Vol. 39, No. 9, Dec. 1976, p. 36.

Table II.9

Distribution of Federal, State and Local Transfer Benefits to Families Classified by Pre-tax/Pre-transfer Income Quintiles Fiscal Year 1976

Quintiles[(a)]	Social insurance[(b)]	Cash Assistance[(c)]	In-kind transfers I[(d)]	In-kind transfers II[(e)]
Low 20%	31.9	61.5	47.6	53.2
Second 20%	28.4	20.5	31.2	26.5
Third 20%	16.2	9.2	12.2	10.5
Fourth 20%	12.0	5.0	5.5	5.4
High 20%	11.5	3.8	3.5	4.5
Total	100.0%	100%	100.0%	100%
Total dollars in billions	$124.0	$18.0	$9.6	$41.4

Source: Congress of the United States, Congressional Budget Office: Poverty Status of Families Under Alternative Definitions of Income (Congressional Budget Office, Background Paper No. 17 (Revised), Washington, D.C., June 1977), p. 4.

(a) The upper limits of each quintile are as follows: low 20% ($1,812), second 20% ($7,871), third 20% ($13,994), and fourth quintile ($21,682).

(b) Social insurance covers social security and railroad retirement, government pensions, unemployment insurance, workers compensation, and veterans' compensation.

(c) Cash assistance covers veterans' pensions, Supplemental Security Income (SSI) and Aid to Families with Dependent Children (AFDC). It does not include state general assistance.

(d) In-kind transfer under group I covers food stamps, childrens nutrition and housing assistance.

(e) In-kind transfers under group II covers Medicare (hospital insurance and supplemental medical insurance) and Medicaid.

The following discussion of the effects of cash transfers and those of in-kind transfers is based on the findings of the Plotnick-Skidmore study and the Congressional Budget Office study referred to above.

The effects of cash transfers

As shown in Chapter 1, according to the Plotnick-Skidmore estimates the impact of public cash transfers on poverty reduction was substantial and growing over the period 1965 to 1972. As a result of cash transfers the proportion of the pre-transfer poverty population lifted above the official poverty line increased from 27 per cent in 1965 to 38 per cent in 1972. Counted by families (including unrelated individuals) the corresponding percentage rose from 33 per cent to 44 per cent.

Of equal interest were the effects of cash transfers on different groups of pre-transfer poverty population as well as the relative effects of different types of cash transfers. On these aspects the Plotnick-Skidmore findings on the four demographic groups and the three types of cash transfer programmes are reproduced in table II.10. The main findings are discussed briefly below.

1. Among the four demographic groups families with aged heads (65 years and over), which formed nearly half of the total number of pre-transfer poor families, derived the greatest benefits from public cash transfers. Between 1965 and 1972 the proportion of pre-transfer poor families with aged heads thereby kept above the poverty line increased from 51 per cent to 63 per cent. For the three non-aged groups the effects of public cash transfers were rather limited. In 1972, the percentage of non-aged pre-transfer poor families lifted above the poverty line by cash transfers was 26 per cent among those with no children and 23 per cent, respectively, among male-headed families with children and among female-headed families with children. In other words, after cash transfers about three-quarters of the pre-transfer poor families were still in poverty. Compared to the condition in 1965 the rate of poverty reduction had risen appreciably among the other two non-aged groups but not among pre-transfer poor non-aged female-headed families with children.

2. Though not targeted on the poverty population, social security (Old-age, Survival and Disability Insurance) was by far the largest single contributor to poverty reduction. It accounted for 64 per cent of total pre-transfer families made non-poor by all cash transfers in 1965 and for 70 per cent in 1972. Significantly, social security not only had powerful anti-poverty effect on the aged. Its effects on poor families with non-aged heads and with no children and those with non-aged male heads with children were actually greater than those of cash transfers under public assistance. Next ranked other non-public-assistance cash transfers. Their relative importance fell, however, from 27 per cent in 1965 to 18 per cent in 1972. Cash transfers under public assistance proved to be the least effective although public assistance aimed specifically at poverty alleviation. Even for non-aged female-headed families with children only half (12 per cent) of the 23 per cent of these families taken out of

Table II.10 Number of Pre-transfer Poor Families[a] and Percentage Taken out of Absolute Poverty by Public Cash Transfers, by Demographic Groups: 1965 and 1972 (Number in thousands)

	Pre-transfer Poor households		Percentage made non-poor by social security(b)		Additional percentage made non-poor by other non-public assistance transfers(c)		Additional percentage made non-poor by public assistance transfers(d)		Total percentage made non-poor by all cash transfers	
	1965	1972	1965	1972	1965	1972	1965	1972	1965	1972
All families	15 609	17 640	21	30	9	8	3	5	33	44
Families with aged heads[e]	7 512	8 643	36	51	12	7	3	4	51	63
Families with non-aged male heads, with children	2 761	2 011	3	7	7	10	2	6	11	23
Families with non-aged female heads, with children	1 395	2 210	12	9	4	2	6	12	22	23
Families with non-aged heads with no children(f)	3 943	4 776	8	12	9	10	3	4	19	26

Source: Robert D. Plotnick and Felicity Skidmore, *op. cit.*, pp. 146-147. Data from tabulations of the Survey of Economic Opportunity and Current Population Survey Tapes.

(a) Families include unrelated individuals as single-person families.

(b) Old Age, Survivors and Disability Insurance.

(c) Unemployment insurance, Workmen's Compensation, veterans' benefits and government employee pensions.

(d) Old Age Assistance, Aid to the Blind, Aid to the Permanently and Totally Disabled and Aid to Families with Dependent Children.

(e) Includes unrelated individuals.

(f) Most are unrelated individuals, but childless couples are included.

poverty by cash transfers in 1972 can be attributed to public assistance, the remaining half are due to the effects of the other two types of cash transfer programmes. The main reason is that in many states the maximum income that a family can have and still qualify for public assistance and the maximum benefit levels for families with no other income remained below the poverty line. "Hence, even though many needy families received welfare in the 1960s and 1970s, thereby increasing their income, most of them were not taken over the poverty line."[1]

The effects of in-kind transfers

The effects of public in-kind transfers on poverty reduction compared with those of cash transfers were assessed systematically in the Congressional Budget Office study for the fical year 1976. As already noted, the study adopted the following classification of public transfer programmes:

Cash transfers

Cash social insurance: social security (OASDI) and railroad retirement, government pensions, unemployment insurance, workers' compensation, veterans' compensation.

Cash assistance: Veterans' pensions, Supplemental Security Income (SSI) and Aid to Families with Dependent Children (AFDC).

In-kind transfers

Group I: Food stamps, child nutrition and housing assistance.

Group II: Medicare (Hospital Insurance and Supplemental Medical Insurance) and medicaid.

One special feature of the estimating procedures adopted by the study is the use of a statistical model to calculate and distribute benefits under the AFDC and SSI programmes and the food stamp programme to families by applying the accounting rules of the respective programmes to families in the Current Population Survey. Benefits from child nutrition, housing assistance, medicare and medicaid were distributed to broad economic and demographic characteristics of the families specifically eligible for a particular programme.[2] Adjustments were also made

---

[1] Robert D. Plotnick and Felicity Skidmore, op. cit., p. 148.

[2] "Since benefits for each family are calculated according to the accounting rules of the program, they are not necessarily the exact amount received by that family, but are rather the amount the family would have received if there were no administrative discretion exercised or errors in applying program rules." (Congress of the United States, Congressional Budgetary Office: Poverty Status of Families Under Alternative Definitions of Income, op. cit., p. 18.)

for under-reporting and non-reporting of transfer and non-transfer incomes in the Current Population Survey.[1]

For valuation of in-kind transfers, the full government cost was used. "It may be argued that the cash value to the recipient of in-kind transfers is less than the cost to the Government. Therefore, by imputing to families the full cost to the Government, the actual benefit as viewed by the recipient may be overstated."[2]

The estimated effects of public cash transfers and in-kind transfers in reducing poverty are shown in table II.11(a) and (b). The estimates cover not only pre-transfer families living below the official poverty line but also those below 125 per cent and 150 per cent of the official poverty line.

Attention will be drawn first to the following main features regarding those below the official poverty line.

1. In fiscal year 1976, 27 per cent of families (including unrelated individuals as single-person families) had pre-tax/pre-transfer incomes below the official poverty line.[3] As a result of public cash transfers the poverty incidence was reduced from 27 per cent to 13.5 per cent or a reduction in poverty by 50 per cent. If public in-kind transfers were counted as income, the incidence fell to 8.1 per cent or was reduced by 20 per cent. The contribution of cash transfers to poverty reduction was therefore far greater than that of in-kind transfers, the ratio being 2.5 to 1. Among cash transfers social insurance programmes accounted for 60 per cent of reduction in poverty, while cash assistance programmes contributed no more than 11.6 per cent. Among in-kind transfers those in group II, namely, medicare and medicaid, played a more important role than those in group II (AFDC, SSI and veterans' pension).

2. Non-Whites had a markedly higher pre-transfer poverty incidence (44 per cent) than Whites (25 per cent). The extent of poverty reduction brought about by public transfers was, however, smaller for non-Whites than for Whites. After cash and in-kind transfers the poverty incidence for non-Whites decreased from

---

[1] For a description of the technical procedures, see Mathematica Policy Research: Analysis of Current Income Maintenance Programs and Budget Alternatives, Fiscal Years 1976, 1978 and 1982: Technical Documentation and Basic Output, Mar. 1977, cited in Poverty Status of Families Under Alternative Definitions of Income, op. cit., p. 17.

[2] Poverty Status of Families Under Alternative Definitions of Income, op. cit., p. 19.

[3] For fiscal year 1976 the official poverty line was estimated at $5,674 for a male-headed non-farm family of four. For a table of estimated official poverty lines for fiscal year 1976 by family size and sex of heads, by farm or non-farm residence, see Poverty Status of Families Under Alternative Definitions of Income, op. cit., p. 23.

Table II.11 (a)

Total Number and Incidence of Families[a] Below 100 per cent, 125 per cent and 150 per cent of Official Poverty Line in Fiscal Year 1976

	Below 100 per cent	Below 125 per cent	Below 150 per cent
Number in pre-transfer poverty (pre-tax) (in thousands)	21 437	24 272	27 164
Pre-tax/pre-transfer poverty incidence (in %)	27.0	30.6	34.2
Cash transfers			
Social insurance[b]	15.7	20.2	24.6
Cash assistance[c] added	13.5	18.5	23.4
In-kind transfers			
In-kind group I[d] added	11.3	17.2	22.6
In-kind group II[e] added	8.1	12.9	18.0
Total reduction in poverty incidence	-18.9	-17.7	-16.2
Percentage reduction	-70.0	-57.8	-47.4

Source: Congress of the United States, Congressional Budget Office: Poverty Status of Families Under Alternative Definitions of Income (Congressional Budget Office, Background Paper No. 17 (Revised), Washington, D.C., June 1977), p. 25.

(a) Families are defined to include unrelated individuals as one-person families.

(b) Cash social insurance includes social security and railroad retirement, government pensions, unemployment insurance, workers' compensation and veterans' compensation.

(c) Cash assistance includes veterans' pensions, Supplemental Security Income, and Aid to Families with Dependent Children.

(d) In-kind transfers group I includes food stamps, child nutrition and housing assistance.

(e) In-kind transfers group II includes medicare (hospital insurance and supplemental medical insurance) and medicaid.

Table II.11 (b)

Number and Incidence of Families Below 100 per cent, 125 per cent and 150 per cent of the Official Poverty Line by Race, Age of Family Head, and Family Type in Fiscal Year 1976

	Below 100 per cent		Below 125 per cent		Below 150 per cent	
	By Race					
	Non-white	White	Non-white	White	Non-white	White
Number of families (in thousands)	4 106	17 330	4 561	19 711	5 025	22 139
Pre-tax/pre-transfer incidence (%)	43.8	24.7	48.6	28.2	53.5	31.7
Cash transfers						
social insurance	33.6	13.3	40.7	17.5	46.9	21.6
cash assistance added	28.9	11.4	37.2	16.1	44.7	20.7
In-kind transfers						
In-kind group I added	22.7	9.8	33.9	14.8	42.8	19.8
In-kind group II added	15.9	7.1	26.3	11.1	36.4	15.6
Total reduction in incidence	-27.9	-17.6	-22.3	-17.1	-17.1	-16.1
Percentage reduction	-63.7	-71.3	-45.9	-60.1	-30.0	-50.8
	By Age of Family Head					
	Aged(a)	Non-aged	Aged	Non-aged	Aged	Non-aged
Number of families (in thousands)	9,647	11,789	10,370	13,903	11,000	16,166
Pre-tax/pre-transfer incidence (%)	59.9	18.7	64.4	22.0	68.3	25.6
Cash transfers						
social insurance	21.5	14.2	30.6	17.6	38.2	21.1
cash assistance added	16.7	12.7	26.3	16.6	36.1	20.3
In-kind transfers						
In-kind group I added	14.0	10.7	24.3	15.4	34.7	19.6
In-kind group II added	6.1	8.6	12.4	13.0	19.6	17.6
Total reduction in incidence	-53.8	-10.1	-52.0	-9.0	-48.7	-8.0
Percentage reduction	-89.8	-54.0	-80.7	-40.9	-71.3	-31.2
	By Family Type					
	Single-person	Multiple-person	Single-person	Multiple-person	Single-person	Multiple-person
Number of families (in thousands)	10,306	11,130	11,244	13,021	12,058	15,100
Pre-tax/pre-transfer incidence (%)	47.8	19.3	52.2	22.6	56.0	26.2
Cash transfers						
social insurance	28.5	10.9	37.1	14.0	43.9	17.5
cash assistance added	25.0	9.2	34.3	12.6	42.8	16.2
In-kind transfers						
In-kind group I added	23.1	6.9	32.6	11.4	41.7	15.5
In-kind group II added	16.5	4.9	23.7	8.8	31.2	13.0
Total reduction in incidence	-31.3	-14.4	-28.5	-13.8	-24.8	-13.2
Percentage reduction	-65.5	-74.6	-54.6	-61.1	-44.3	-50.4

Source: Congress of the United States, Congressional Budget Office: *Poverty Status of Families Under Alternative Definitions of Income*, op. cit., pp. 26-31.

(a) Aged = 65 years and over.

44 per cent to 16 per cent or a reduction by 64 per cent, whereas that for Whites decreased from 25 per cent to 7 per cent or a reduction by 71 per cent. Since benefits from social insurance programmes were mostly wage-related and since the average wage for non-Whites was considerably lower than the average wage for Whites, a much greater proportion of non-White poor families received social insurance benefits too low to keep them above the poverty line. Thus, only 37 per cent of pre-transfer non-White poor families were lifted over the poverty line by social insurance compared with 65 per cent for Whites. They had to rely far more on cash assistance and in-kind transfers than did Whites. In-kind transfers I and II accounted for 47 per cent of poverty reduction among non-Whites compared with 24 per cent among Whites.

3. Families with aged heads (65 years and over) formed as much as 45 per cent of pre-transfer families below the official poverty line. After public transfers their poverty incidence showed a dramatic decline to 6 per cent or a reduction by 90 per cent. Social insurance alone accounted for 71 per cent of poverty reduction in this demographic group and medicare for another 15 per cent. The remaining 14 per cent was attributable to cash assistance and in-kind transfers in group I. In contrast, families with non-aged heads had a pre-transfer poverty incidence of not more than 19 per cent. Public transfers brought the incidence down to 8.6 per cent, which was slightly higher than the corresponding poverty incidence among families with aged heads. Roughly 60 per cent of poverty reduction in the non-aged group can be traced to cash transfers and 40 per cent to in-kind transfers.

4. Strikingly enough, nearly half of pre-transfer families below the official poverty line were single person families, i.e. counted as unrelated individuals. A large proportion of persons in this group were aged persons; to that extent, this group overlaps the "families with aged heads" group. The remainder of this group consisted largely of young persons. The pre-transfer poverty incidence among single-person families was exceedingly high - about 48 per cent. After public transfers the incidence fell to 16.5 per cent or a reduction by 65 per cent which was smaller compared to multiple-person families. Among multiple-person families the pre-transfer poverty incidence was much lower - 19 per cent, but the extent of poverty reduction was greater. The poverty incidence after public transfers decreased to about 5 per cent or a reduction of 75 per cent. In both demographic groups - single-person families and multiple-person families - approximately 70 per cent of poverty reduction was due to cash transfers and 30 per cent due to in-kind transfers. Over half of the poverty reduction in both groups resulted from social insurance alone.

5. According to the Congressional Budget Study, if in-kind transfers are counted as income and taxes (federal personal income and employee taxes and state income taxes) are excluded from income, over the decade between 1965 and fiscal year 1976, the over-all incidence of poverty among families, thus estimated, has been reduced by roughly 56 per cent, in contrast to the more modest

reduction - about 28 per cent - derived from the Census Bureau's poverty statistics based on a money income concept which excludes in-kind transfers but includes taxes.[1]

When consideration is extended to families whose pre-transfer incomes were below 125 per cent and 150 per cent respectively of the official poverty line, the following findings from the Congressional Budget Office estimates for fiscal year 1976 are of interest especially from the point of view of raising absolute poverty standards.

1. Each 25 per cent increase over the official poverty line was roughly associated with 3.6 per cent increase in the over-all pre-transfer poverty incidence and an increase of 3 million families in pre-transfer poverty. Thus by raising the poverty standard from the official poverty line successively to 125 per cent and 150 per cent of the official poverty line, the pre-transfer poverty for all families would increase from 27 per cent successively to 30.6 per cent and 34.2 per cent, and the total number of families in pre-transfer poverty correspondingly from 21.4 million to 24.3 million and 27.2 million. Among various demographic groups the increase was greater for those with a lower pre-transfer poverty incidence. This is particularly noticeable for families with non-aged heads compared with those with aged heads and for multiple-person families compared with single-person families. Between Whites and non-Whites the difference in the rate of increase was, however, appreciably smaller.

2. The impact of the public transfer programmes, each and all, diminished steadily with rises in the poverty standard. As the poverty standard increased from the official poverty line to 25 per cent and 50 per cent above, the extent of poverty reduction resulting from public transfers fell from 70 per cent to 58 per cent and 48 per cent. The over-all post-transfer poverty incidence increased successively from 8 per cent to 13 and 18 per cent. Among various demographic groups it is noteworthy that the post-transfer poverty incidence for non-Whites rose from 16 per cent to 26 per cent and 36 per cent; and for single-person families, from 16 per cent to 24 and 31 per cent.

3. At higher poverty standards the relative effect of the public transfer programmes in reducing poverty continued to be greater for Whites than for non-Whites; for multiple-person families than for single-person families, and for families with aged heads than for those with non-aged heads.

4. With rises in poverty standard cash transfers still accounted for over two-thirds of poverty reduction. However, their relative importance was decreasing, whereas in-kind transfers were gaining in importance. Among cash transfers social insurance continued to retain its predominant role, while

---

[1] Congress of the United States, Congressional Budget Office; Poverty Status of Families Under Alternative Definitions of Income, op. cit., p. 9.

the part played by cash assistance dwindled. Similarly, among in-kind transfer programmes, medicare and medicaid took on increasing importance, while the effects of in-kind transfers in group II decreased rapidly at higher poverty standards. Social insurance coupled with medicare and medicaid accounted for 77 per cent of poverty reduction at the official poverty standard; 83 per cent at 125 per cent of the official standard, and 88 per cent at 150 per cent of the official standard. Equally significant, the relative contribution of cash assistance and in-kind transfers in group II combined fell correspondingly from 23 per cent to 17 per cent and 12 per cent.

Drawbacks of the programmes

As a general conclusion it can be said that the income maintenance programmes did succeed in lifting a large proportion of the pre-transfer poor population above a low absolute poverty standard as officially defined. Its success can be attributed chiefly to the enormous size of fiscal expenditure allotted to income maintenance as already shown, but, in retrospect, partly also to the gradual emergence of what might be called a three-tier income maintenance system, namely, social insurance plus cash public assistance plus in-kind public assistance.

The three-tier system, however, contains various drawbacks some of which were indicated in the previous discussion of individual programmes. Indeed, the literature on poverty policy in the United States was replete with criticisms of this system and with proposals for reform. As is well recognised, the multiplicity of income maintenance programmes now in existence was the outcome of piece-meal and unco-ordinated growth of separate programmes in response to different needs and pressures coming to the fore over the past decades. Many of the drawbacks of the present system can be traced to its historical setting, while some other appear to be rooted in the concept of deserving public aid applied to different groups of the poverty population. In what follows its major drawbacks are briefly reviewed.

Specific programmes

Under the income maintenance system described above poor households were treated differently according to the category in which they belonged. Categorisation of the poor originated in the conception of the degree to which aid was "deserved" which was in turn guided by the "employability" of the poor. Thus, in the most favoured category were the aged, the disabled and the blind. Less favoured was the category consisting of families with children mostly headed by women or, less frequently, by unemployed fathers. The least favoured category comprised what had come to be known as the working poor - the non-aged, non-disabled working male family heads with dependent children, childless couples and unrelated individuals. The working poor were generally not eligible for income maintenance programmes open to the other two categories except for general assistance and food stamps, even though the earnings from their work were very low and lower than the benefits received by many households in the other two categories. To correct this source of inequality in the system has been a main object of reform.

Low average cash benefits

Among the poor eligible for cash transfer programmes the average cash benefits were low measured by the poverty line income. Even for old-age benefits, which included relatively high benefits paid to beneficiaries with high previous earnings, the average monthly benefits in 1975 were $312 (including allowance for one dependant) equivalent to 115 per cent of the poverty line for a two-person family with an aged male head (65 years and over). Since the amount of old-age benefits received varied directly with the recipient's previous earnings, large numbers of retired workers, whose previous earnings had been much below the average if living on their old-age pension alone, would fall below the poverty line even after the earnings replacement rate had been raised. The minimum old-age benefits for a couple in July 1974 was 57 per cent of the corresponding poverty line. The income position of recipients of low old-age benefits, however, had been improved by the Federal Supplemental Security income performance introduced in 1974. By comparison, the average weekly benefits under state unemployment insurance programmes were $70 equivalent to no more than 66 per cent of the poverty line income for a four-person non-farm family on an annual basis. Like social security benefits, unemployment benefits were wage-related. For unemployed workers whose previous wages were below the average their unemployment benefits could be much less than one-half of the poverty line income especially in states which provided no dependants' supplement. The inadequacy of unemployment benefits would be felt most acutely among the former low-wage earners in long-term unemployment and with children. This appeared to be the main reason for the June 1975 Supreme Court decision which allows unemployed fathers who are eligible for unemployment benefits to receive instead higher benefits under AFDC-UF programme. While the benefits under AFDC programme varied according to the size of family and the recipients who automatically were eligible for various in-kind transfer programmes, the average AFDC cash benefits were equally low. In December 1975 the average monthly cash payment per recipient under AFDC programme was $72.45 equivalent to about 64 per cent of the poverty line income for a four-person family headed by a woman.

The above figures of the average cash benefits under the important cash transfer programmes already cited earlier in this chapter, were assembled here only to bring into sharper relief the fact that for each programme taken separately, the average cash benefits were so low that those living on benefits at the average level and with no other income would fall far below the poverty line in the case of AFDC and unemployment benefits, and the same would happen to the retired workers whose old-age benefits were only moderately below the average.

Wide inter-state disparities

The discussion of average benefits has concealed wide inter-state disparities. Nearly all the state administered programmes financed partly or wholly from state and local funds displayed wide differences in eligibility requirements and benefit levels. As a rule, in the poor states in the south where the poverty incidence was high and where a large proportion of Black poverty population was located the benefit levels were very much lower than those prevailing in the rich states. The striking inter-state disparities in maximum AFDC payment standards and in medicaid payment per recipient were discussed earlier in this chapter. The differences in the level of unemployment benefit may be cited as another example. In May 1976 the average weekly unemployment benefit varied from about $49 in Mississippi, $55 in Texas and $57 in West Virginia to $88 in Pennsylvania, $91 in Illinois and $99 in the District of Columbia.[1]

One consequence of wide inter-state disparities in eligibility requirements and benefit level was the migration of the poor from the poor states to the richer states, thus aggravating the overcrowding of the ghetto and slum population in the central cities of the rich states. In many cases the latter again prompted the richer people in the central cities to move out to the suburban areas, contributing to the erosion of tax base of central cities, which in turn affected adversely the size of welfare schemes run by localities.

The wide inter-state disparities in income maintenance programmes can be ascribed, to a large measure, to the differences in the revenue position between poor states and rich states. However, as shown by a study of the earlier experience with medicaid previously referred to, federal encouragement of poor states to increase their expenditure on public assistance by such devices as specially favourable federal reimbursement formulas did not lead to desired effects. The study concludes that "in sum, the Medicaid program raises a host of new questions of the wisdom involved in continued reliance on joint federal - state welfare policy. If we consider equity a primary goal of public assistance, then we can purchase improvement only at the price of 100 per cent federal financing of all welfare programs".[2]

The built-in work disincentives

Since the level of cash benefits was low in many states, the growth of in-kind benefits as a supplement appeared to be a desirable, if not an ideal, step in the evolution of the income maintenance system. Indeed, as shown above, in-kind transfers contributed significantly to the reduction of poverty. However, the manner in which they were incorporated into the system has led to a structural change in the form of payment of multiple benefits taking on increasing importance in the 1970s.

---

[1] US Department of Health, Education and Welfare, Social Administration: Social Security Bulletin, Vol. 39, No. 11, Nov. 1976, table M-38, p. 80.

[2] Bruce C. Stuart: "The Impact of Medicaid on Interstate Income Differentials", in Kenneth E. Boulding and Martin Pfaff: Redistribution to the Rich and the Poor, op. cit., p. 168.

Participation of a poor household in multiple transfer programmes - in cash as well as in kind - by increasing their total real benefits should be a good thing in the absence of any better arrangement. But as the practice has grown, it has unwittingly built into the system disincentives to work effort despite the recipient's preference of work to welfare.

While empirical evidence remains to be ascertained regarding the actual prevalence of these disincentives, the sources of these disincentives have been identified. These were discussed at some length earlier in this chapter and only need to be briefly recapitulated. The first was the high cumulative benefit reduction rate accompanying an increase in earned income. Though for each programme taken separately the benefit reduction rate may be low in order to encourage work, the cumulative benefit reductions from all the programmes in which the poor household had participated as an increase in earned income could yield an exceedingly high marginal tax rate on earned income which could virtually inhibit all incentives to work. As noted previously, it was not uncommon for a poor household participating in multiple programmes to face a marginal tax rate as high as 85 per cent or even higher. The second and even more serious was the "income notch" effect: the sudden complete cessation of payment of benefits from all programmes as soon as the earned income reached the break-even point or the maximum payment standard. At that point the loss in benefits could well exceed the disposable income earned (after taxes and work expenses). The crucial deterrent to greater work effort and higher earnings in this connection was the loss of free medicaid which could be a financial disaster to the household. This also testifies to the unsoundness of the medicaid programme in operation and the need for drastic reform.

The widespread practice of receiving multiple benefits among the recipients of specific assistance also tended to accentuate inequalities in the public transfer system. Examples of this can be found in the earlier discussion. There was a general awareness of this drawback of the transfer system. However, appropriate measures to secure the needed improvements are still being developed taking especially into account the importance of guarding against "averaging down" the benefits.

Administrative complexity

The administration of public transfer programmes in the United States has been extremely complex. The complexity stemmed partly from the unco-ordinated growth of different programmes but partly from divided responsibility of the Federal, state and local governments for financing, legislating and managing different programmes. This resulted in a loss in efficiency and in a lack of unified effort to attain certain clearly defined national goals in this field.

As a brief description of the administrative complexities involved, one can do no better than to quote the following statement by the Sub-committee on Fiscal Policy of the Joint Economic Committee of US Congress:[1]

"The local welfare agency's work is supervised by many offices:

HEW (The Department of Health, Education and Welfare) and state welfare agency supervise AFDC.
HEW supervises SSI.
HEW, often with the state health department, regulates medicaid.
The Agriculture Department and the state welfare agency supervise the food stamp and food commodity programs.
The Labour Department regulates the state employment service, which participates in enforcing work rules of AFDC and food program.
The Department of Housing and Urban Department oversees welfare operations like model cities, homemaker services, and housing aid to the aged.
State and local governments control general assistance, which they finance.
State civil service regulations govern agency personal policies.

Eligibility rules for need-based programmes are complex and difficult to enforce; benefit compensation almost invites mistakes. Intricate payment policies confuse applicants and case-workers, prevent needy persons from knowing their eligibility, cause some to drop out of the application process in frustration and waste time of others, and flood case-workers with paper work."

Stigma

In the United States "to admit to being poor is almost synonymous with an admission of failure".[2] To be a recipient of public assistance one had to go through the means test or income test. The passing of the means test was a stigma - a label of being poor. People generally detested it. Moreover, the recipients were subjected to close supervision by the case-workers. The latter frequently checked upon the clients' way of spending the welfare money and their private lives to make sure that the clients did not step beyond the conditions laid down for them while on welfare. This was particularly true of the AFDC programme. It was observed that "a large portion of the case-worker-client relation, which should be one of warm co-operation,

---

[1] 93rd US Congress, 2nd Session, Joint Economic Committee: Income Security for Americans: Recommendations of the Public Welfare Study: Report of the Sub-committee on Fiscal Policy of the Joint Economic Committee, op. cit., pp. 80-81.

[2] Irwin Garfinkel: "An Overview Paper", in Michael B. Barth, George J. Carcagno and John L. Palmer: Toward an Effective Income Support System: Problems, Prospects and Choices, op. cit., pp. 163-164.

has turned into an adversary one characterised by concealment, snooping, personal indignity and domination, and chiseling".[1] Even for the food stamp programme, the most liberal of all the means tested programmes, it was suspected that "the desire to avoid this labelling effect may be one of the reasons that so many of the working poor are not claiming the food stamp benefits to which they are entitled."

The drawbacks of the income maintenance programmes reviewed above are perhaps the most widely discussed in literature on welfare reform policy in the United States. They make it clear that there is a great need for improvement of the existing income maintenance system. A great number of options have been suggested for change, and although each has its own particular provisions, they all tend to be built on five particular tenets:

(a) Any new arrangements for income maintenance programmes should keep to the absolute minimum any increase in required budgetary allocations. There is, and always has been, a bias against increasing welfare expenditures in the US, and such a limitation on increases would work to make a scheme more acceptable politically.

(b) There should be a simplification of the system in the sense that a single basic federal cash income support payment should replace the current rather cumbersome system made up of many different income support programmes. The current system includes, for example, aid to families with dependent children (AFDC), supplemental security income (SSI) and food stamps. Furthermore, the existing programmes fall within the jurisdiction of 9 Federal Executive Departments, 21 Congressional Committees, 54 state welfare agencies and more than 3,000 local welfare offices.

(c) Work should be made more profitable than welfare. That is, there should be less than a 100 per cent decrease in welfare benefits for each dollar earned which would only reach 100 per cent progressively and at a pre-determined income much above the full-income support level. Within the current system, for example, there is the possibility that a man with a wife and two children living in Ohio could double his earnings from \$2,600 to \$5,200 but, due to decreases in AFDC and food stamps and an increase in work related expenses, his net annual income would increase by only \$178, and he and his family lose eligibility for medicaid (normally worth several hundred dollars per year on average).[2]

---

[1] Joseph K. Kershaw: Government Against Poverty (The Brookings Institution, Washington, D.C., 1970), p. 103.

[2] See US Department of Health, Education and Welfare, Report on the 1977 Welfare Reform Study (Washington: USHEW, 1977), pp. 10-11.

(d) Any variation between benefits received in different states should be based on true and documented differences in the cost of living, and machinery should be set up to gather and analyse information relating to differences in the cost of living. A family of four residing in Kansas City, Missouri, presently is eligible for $2,040 per year in AFDC benefits, whereas, if they moved across the river to Kansas City, Kansas, the benefits would rise to $3,672. The same comparison for Texas and Oklahoma yields figures of $1,680 and $3,408 respectively.[1]

(e) A requirement that needs to be enforced vigourously is that all those receiving benefits and in a position to work must accept available employment. This will entail complementary efforts at the creation of public service jobs and training of the unskilled. Efforts should be made to make employment in the private sector preferable to the public sector, e.g., an increase in the earned income tax credit.

All options which are proposed so as to reform the welfare system need to be analysed in terms of how well they fulfill these five tenets.

Chapter 3

Taxation and redistribution

The preceding chapter focused on the fiscal expenditures for poverty alleviation and, in particular, on public transfers under the income maintenance programmes. It was shown that with all their defects these expenditures did produce a significant overall impact on the reduction of pre-transfer poverty. This, however, is only half the picture. It remains to consider the effects on absolute and relative poverty of the tax system.

Taxes in the United States are a broad and complex subject. In this chapter attention will be confined to certain drawbacks of the tax system which either place a heavy tax burden on the poor or accord favourable tax treatment to the rich, and to certain proposals for tax reform, especially proposals for a negative income tax.

The structure of the tax system

In order to gain a proper perspective, the size of tax revenue and the structure of the tax system in the United States are briefly reviewed below.

In 1973 the tax revenue of Federal, state and local governments combined (including "social insurance taxes and contributions") totalled $363 billion as shown in table III.1. This amount formed about 28 per cent of the gross national product. At that level the total tax burden in the United States was appreciably lower than in most other developed countries. A comparison of 15 developed countries has shown that in 1972 the United States ranked twelfth (see table III.2).

Of the total tax revenue in 1973 the Federal Government accounted for 63 per cent ($230 billion), and state and local governments together for 37 per cent ($133 billion). Excluding "social insurance taxes and contributions", the total tax revenue was distributed as follows: ederal overnment, 57.7 per cent ($165.5 billion); state governments, 23.8 per cent ($68.1 billion); and local governments, 18.5 per cent ($53 billion).

The tax structure differed markedly as between the Federal, state and local governments. For federal tax revenue direct taxes were of predominant importance. Including "social insurance taxes and contributions" direct taxes represented 88.6 per cent of the federal tax revenue in 1973 as against 11.4 per cent from indirect taxes. Among the direct taxes the principal features were the large shares assumed by individual income taxes (44.8 per cent) and "social insurance taxes and contributions" (28.1 per cent) and the minor role of corporation taxes (15.7 per cent).

"Social insurance taxes and contributions" were relatively unimportant in the tax revenue of state and local governments. The tax revenue of state governments (not including "social insurance taxes and contributions") came primarily from indirect

Table III.1 Tax Revenue: All Governments in 1973 (in billions of dollars)

Total	All governments		Federal		State and local: Total		State and local: State		State and local: Local	
	Amount	% distri-bution	Amount	% distri-bution	Amount	% distri-bution	Amount	% distri-bution	Amount	% distri-bution
Excluding social insurance taxes and contributions	286.6		165.5		121.1		68.1	100%	53.0	100%
Including social insurance taxes and contributions	363.3	100%	230.1	100%	133.2	100%	(a)		(a)	
Social insurance taxes and contributions[1]	76.7	21.1	64.6	28.1	12.1[(2)]	9.1	(a)		(a)	
Individual income	121.2	33.4	103.2	44.8	18.0	13.5	15.6	22.9	2.4	4.5
Corporation income	41.6	11.4	36.2	15.7	5.4	4.1	5.4	7.9	(b)	
Sales, gross receipts[(3)]	61.8	17.0	19.7	8.6	42.0	31.5	37.1	54.5	4.9	9.2
Property	45.3	12.5	(c)	(c)	45.3	34.0	1.3	1.9	44.0	83.0
Other taxes[(4)]	16.7	4.6	6.4	2.8	10.3	7.7	8.6	12.6	1.7	3.2

Source: Unless otherwise stated, figures are from US Department of Commerce, Bureau of the Census: Statistical Abstract of the United States: 1975 (Washington D.C., 1975, table No. 416, p. 252. (a) Not given in the tables from which the other figures were taken; (b) corporation included with individual incomes; (c) not applicable.

(1) Figures for social insurance taxes and contributions are from the following tables from Statistical Abstract of the United States: 1975: for all governments, figures for "insurance trust" in table No. 417, p. 253; for Federal Government from table No. 372 on federal budget, p. 226 (sum of employment taxes and contributions ($54.9 billion), unemployment insurance ($6.1 billion) and other contributions ($3.6 billion)).

(2) The figure of $12.1 billion was obtained by subtracting from the figure for all governments ($76.7 billion) the figure for Federal Government ($64.6 billion).

(3) Federal taxes include customs.

(4) Includes licences.

Table III.2 Taxes as a Percent of Gross National Product and Distribution of Revenues by Major Tax Source, Selected Countries, 1972 [(a)]

Country	Taxes as a percent of GNP	Percentage distribution by major tax source					
		Individual income	Corporation income	Payrolls	Goods and services [(b)]	Property	Death and gift
Norway	45.7	27	2	27	41	2	*
Denmark	44.8	48	2	8	38	4	*
Sweden	43.9	42	4	23	30	1	*
Netherlands	41.8	28	7	35	28	2	*
Austria	37.0	23	4	33	38	2	*
Germany	36.0	28	5	34	30	2	*
France	35.8	11	6	41	40	1	1
Belgium	35.2	27	7	30	34	...	1
United Kingdom	34.7	32	7	18	30	11	2
Canada	33.5	34	11	9	34	11	1
Italy	31.1	13	7	39	39	1	1
United States	28.1	34	11	20	19	13	2
Australia	24.3	38	16	4	34	6	2
Switzerland	24.1	33	8	23	28	6	1
Japan	21.1	26	24 [(c)]	19	24 [(c)]	5	2

Source: Organisation for Economic Co-operation and Development, Revenue Statistics of OECD Member Countries, 1965-1972 (Paris: OECD, 1975). Data are on a calendar year basis for all countries except Denmark and Canada (year begins 1 April) and the United States and Australia (year begins 1 July). Figures are rounded.

* Less than 0.5 per cent.

(a) Includes national and local taxes.
(b) Includes net revenues of utilities and liquor stores, receipts from licences, fees and other charges, stamp taxes on transfers of property and securities, and other transactions taxes paid by enterprises.
(c) The Japanese enterprise tax levied by prefectural governments is included in the corporation income tax and excluded from the tax on goods and services.

taxes (67 per cent) which consisted largely of sales taxes (54.5 per cent), but the role of individual income tax has also been increasing.[1]

The local governments, on the other hand, depended for the most part on one single type of direct tax, namely property tax. This alone accounted for 83 per cent of their tax revenue in 1973.

It is also significant that over the past decade the state and local tax revenues combined have been rising more rapidly than federal tax revenue. Thus, their share in the total tax revenue of all governments increased from 32 per cent in 1960 to 37 per cent in 1970 and 42 per cent in 1973, while the share of federal tax revenue fell correspondingly from 68 per cent to 63 per cent and 58 per cent.[2]

This over-all picture of the tax system provides a backdrop for a discussion of certain of its drawbacks with respect to the alleviation of poverty.

Drawbacks of the system

The two aspects of the tax system considered here are the heavy taxation of the poor and favourable treatment of the rich. These two aspects combined to reduce further the inadequate disposable incomes of the poor and, contrariwise, boost the large disposable incomes of the rich.

Heavy taxation of the poor

The poor bear a heavy tax burden due principally to a combination of three regressive taxes - the payroll taxes levied by Federal Government, the sales taxes by state governments and property tax by local governments. While those whose incomes were below the poverty line had been virtually relieved of payment of income tax since the adoption of the low-income allowance in 1971, these three kinds of taxes were still acting to reduce further their already low levels of real income.

1. The payroll taxes

The taxes bearing most directly on the incomes of families and persons at or below the poverty line were the payroll taxes which are referred to as "social insurance taxes and contributions". As already shown in Chapter 2, the main groups of social insurance in the United States were OASDHI and unemployment insurance,

---

[1] "The states derive the largest share of their tax revenue from general and selective taxes on sales and gross receipts (54.7 per cent of all state tax revenues in 1974). The occasional 1 per cent increases in sales taxes have not been sufficient to offset the accelerating costs of state governments. As a result, the number of states that have turned to personal incomes as an additional source of revenue has increased from 37 in 1969 to 44 in 1974." (David H. Freedman: "Inflation in the United States, 1959-74", in International Labour Review, Vol. 112, Nos. 2-5, Aug.-Sep. 1975, p. 142).

[2] Figures from Statistical Abstract of the United States: 1975, p. 248.

although the former far exceeded the latter in the amount of funds collected. In the case of OASDHI the funds were paid partly by employees and partly by employers, whereas for unemployment insurance the funds were paid wholly by employers (except in a few states).

The part paid by the employee and deducted from his wage is generally recognised as a tax borne by the employee. There had been much discussion of whether and to what extent the incidence of the employer's contribution can be shifted backward to the workers in the form of lower wages or forward to consumers in the form of higher prices. More recently there appears to be general agreement among economists that the employers' contributions are borne by the workers. A recent extensive cross-country empirical investigation has demonstrated this.[1] The study revealed that given the level of productivity in a country, the imposition of a payroll tax tends to reduce the wage rate in dollars by roughly the amount of the tax. As the author has pointed out, while this result could be due to backward or forward shifting or a combination of both, in either case the full burden of the tax falls on workers.

Viewed in this light, the burden of payroll taxes on low earners had been increasing steadily over the past decades. As is shown in table III.3, the OASDHI statutory rates for employee and employer combined rose from 2 per cent in 1949 to 6 per cent in 1960, 9.6 per cent in 1969 and 11.7 per cent in 1975 and 1976, whereas the average contribution rate for state unemployment insurance remained low at 2 per cent. Thus, in 1975 an urban family of four with a single earner living on an annual take-home income of $5,178 would be 6 per cent below the poverty line ($5,500) after having, in fact, paid a payroll tax of $822 (i.e. 13.7 per cent). Without such a tax his earnings ($6,000) would have kept his family 9 per cent above the poverty line. While recent estimates were not readily available, an earlier estimate for the late 1960s indicated that "the Federal Government extracts $1.5 billion of payroll taxes ... from those who are officially classified as poor".[2] By the mid-1970s, compared with individual income tax, the payroll tax was the larger tax for more than half of all wage earners.[3]

The setting of a ceiling on wages and salaries subject to the payroll taxes made these taxes proportionate up to the ceiling and thus increasingly regressive beyond the ceiling. Though the ceiling had been moved upwards, due partly to the raising of the wage level, the regressivity of the payroll taxes remained the same. The ceiling, in fact, granted exemptions to earnings in the upper range. This was particularly true of the low ceiling on unemployment insurance. Furthermore, payroll taxes were levied on wage and salary incomes but not on incomes from property.

---

[1] John A. Brittain: The Payroll Tax for Social Security (The Brookings Institution, Washington D.C., 1972).

[2] Jospeh A. Pechman: "Tax Policies for the 1970s", in Public Policy, Vol. XVIII, No. 1, Autumn 1969, reproduced in Theodore R. Marmor (ed.): Poverty Policy: A Compendium of Cash Transfer Proposals (Aldine-Atherton, Chicago, 1971), p. 219.

[3] George F. Break and Joseph A. Pechman: Federal Tax Reform: The Impossible Dream? (The Brookings Institution, Washington D.C., 1975), p. 107.

Table III.3 OASDHI Statutory Rates and Unemployment Insurance (UI) Rates and their Respective Taxable Ceilings

Year	Taxable ceiling (in dollars) OASDHI	UI	OASDHI statutory rates: employer plus employee (per cent)	Average employer state UI contribution rates (per cent)
1949	$3 000		2	1.3
1955	4 200		4	1.2
1960	4 800		6	1.9
1966	6 600		8.4	1.9
1967	6 600		8.8	1.6
1968	7 800		8.8	1.5
1969	7 800	$3 000(1)	9.6	1.4
1973	12 600(2)	4 200(3)	11.0(2)	2.0(4)
1974	13 200(5)		11.7(5)	
1975	14 300(6)		11.7(6)	
1976	15 300(6)		11.7(6)	

Source: Unless otherwise stated, figures are from John A. Brittain: The Payroll Tax for Social Security (The Brookings Institution, Washington D.C., 1972), Appendix C, p. 270.

(1) Figures from John A. Brittain, op. cit., p. 99.

(2) International Herald Tribune (Paris), 22-23 Dec. 1973, p. 3.

(3) Figures from John A. Brittain, op. cit., p. 88.

(4) Estimated by John A. Brittain.

(5) 93rd US Congress, 2nd Session: Joint Economic Committee: Income Security for Americans: Recommendations of the Public Welfare Study, op. cit., p. 215.

(6) George F. Break and Joseph A. Pechman: Federal Tax Reform: The Impossible Dream? (The Brookings Institution, Washington D.C., 1975), p. 105.

Thus, it is important to stress that the benefits of OASDHI and unemployment insurance transferred to the poor in effect came from a redistribution from wage and salary earners falling primarily within the low end of the income scale. In other words, the public cash transfers that helped lift some of the aged and the disabled out of pre-transfer poverty came mostly from the meagre incomes of the working poor and near-poor, and from the incomes of those workers whose incomes were below the taxable ceiling. The higher incomes beyond the ceiling and the unearned incomes from property were excluded from this redistribution process.

2. Sales and property taxes

The two major types of taxes levied by state and local governments - sales taxes and property tax - have also been criticised for being regressive. Not much material is on hand for a closer analysis of these taxes which will anyway be rendered even more difficult by variations in actual practice among state and local governments.

The general sales tax is regressive because the amount of tax paid by the consumer is in proportion to his total consumption expenditure and because consumption as a proportion of income decreases with increases in income due to increased savings. The incidence of a general sales tax borne by households at the low end of the income scale is expected to be considerably higher than that borne by households at the upper end. For selective sales tax the incidence depends on the commodities or services on the sales of which a tax is levied. Taxes on commodities which have a greater weight in the budget of upper income families are more progressive. The sales tax on a commodity or a service in question could also be proportionate if its relative effects on the budgets of families in different income groups were about the same. The over-all incidence of selective sales taxes in a state is thus determined by the composition of the particular commodities and services subject to sales tax. The burden of these taxes would depend on the height and structure of tax rates levied on these commodities and services.

The property tax imposed by local governments was borne to a large extent by lower to middle-income home owners and by tenants in the form of higher rents - a forward shifting of the property tax paid by landlords (e.g. owners of apartment buildings and tenements in the poor districts). Since housing forms a higher proportion of the budget of a low-income household, property tax is regressive. While systematic analysis of the incidence of this tax in the country was not readily available, a study of the finance of California Government published in 1967 showed that families earning $1,000 per year paid 13 per cent of their income in property taxes, those earning $4,000 to $5,000 a year paid 5 per cent and those with incomes over $15,000 paid only 2 per cent in property taxes.[1] In this case the property tax was very regressive.

---

[1] The finding was from G. Rostvold: Financing California Government (Dickenson Publishing Co., 1967), quoted by Thomas Bodenheimler in his article: "The Poverty of the States", in Monthly Review (New York), Vol. 24, No. 6, Nov. 1972, p. 14.

Though separate estimates of the incidence of each of these two kinds of taxes were difficult to find, some earlier over-all estimates were available regarding the combined tax burden of state and local governments (consisting mainly of sales taxes and property taxes) falling upon families in different income groups. One study found that state and local tax rates in 1965 ranged from 25 per cent for incomes under $2,000 (excluding transfer payments) down to only 7 per cent for incomes above $15,000.[1] Compared with an earlier corresponding estimate of 13 to 5.7 per cent over the same income range for 1958[2] it would appear that the relative burden of state and local taxes upon the poorest group had increased markedly over this seven-year period.

3. The over-all tax burden on the poor

In regard to the over-all tax burden on the poor, one writer stated that:[3]

> While new programs are devised to help the poor, they are required to pay taxes that greatly reduce their ability to make ends meet on their meagre income. The Council of Economic Advisers estimated that in 1965 the average effective rate of taxes paid by those with income below $2,000 was over 40 per cent. Subsequent increases in federal payroll taxes and state-local sales and property taxes have made this burden even heavier.

A systematic analysis of the tax burden at each income level in 1968 was made by Roger A. Harriot and Herman P. Miller using a set of plausible assumptions regarding the incidence of different taxes and adopting a concept of total income which excludes government transfer payments.[4] The study divides the adjusted family money incomes into nine income groups ranging from "under $2,000" to "$50,000 and over". For each income group the federal taxes and state and local taxes paid by the group and the amount of government transfers[5] received by the group were computed as a percentage of the total income of the group.

---

[1] This statement was referred to in Economic Report of the President, Jan. 1969, p. 161, and quoted by John A. Brittain: The Payroll Tax for Social Security, op. cit., p. 87, footnote 10.

[2] Estimate made by R.A. Musgrave in his paper entitled "Calculo de la distribution de la carga tributaria" (Washington D.C., Pan American Union, 1963) cited in Felix Paukert "Social Security and Income Distribution: A Comparative Study", in International Labour Review, Vol. 98, No. 5, Nov. 1968.

[3] Joseph A. Pechman: "Tax Policies for the 1970s", in Public Policy, Vol. XVIII, No. 1, Autumn 1969, reproduced in Theodore R. Marmor (ed.): Poverty Policy: A Compendium of Cash Transfer Proposals, op. cit., p. 219.

[4] Roger A. Harriot and Herman P. Miller: "The Tax We Pay", in Conference Board Record (New York), Vol. III, No. 5, May 1971, pp. 31-40. See in particular table 7 on p. 40.

[5] Government transfer payments in the Harriot-Miller study cover Medicare and Medicaid benefits and all types of money transfers including social security and veterans' benefits, unemployment compensation, public employee retirement and disability payments and public assistance. (Harriot and Miller, op. cit., p. 36.)

The estimated over-all tax rates for different income groups given in the Harriot-Miller study displayed a U-shaped pattern along the income scale.[1] The lowest income group bore the heaviest tax burden amounting to 50 per cent of their total income. Among the second lowest income group the over-all tax rate was 34.6 per cent. Of particular significance is the finding that in 1968, about 47 per cent of the government transfer payments received by the lowest income group was offset by the high taxes they paid and the rate of offset rose to 71 per cent among the second lowest. It should be remembered that many of the poor also paid high taxes but received little or no government transfer payments. As is also shown in the study, while the federal income tax was distinctly progressive, the social security tax was regressive. More striking was the high regressivity of state and local taxes at the lower end of the income scale. Figuring prominently among these were the state sales tax and the local property tax.

With a view to updating the Harriot-Miller study, an attempt was made to estimate the tax rates and transfer rates at each income level in 1970 based on data processed for this purpose by the Brookings Institution at the request of the ILO. The income classes in current dollars used are the same as those used by the Harriot-Miller study; the incidence assumptions are also the same except for the property tax.[2] However, the Brookings data on adjusted family income are based on a broader concept of income which, inter alia, includes government transfer payments.[3] The estimates for 1970 derived from these data are given in table III.4. It may be noted that even measured from a broader income base the estimated over-all tax rate among the lowest income group in 1970 was as high as 86 per cent of their aggregate adjusted family income, and that the amount of taxes they paid was greater than the amount of government transfer payments they received. For the second lowest income group the over-all tax rate declined abruptly to 23.2 per cent but the taxes they paid offset 45 per cent of the government transfer payments they received. Equally significant, the state and local taxes, which, as has been already noted, were highly regressive, accounted for 72 per cent of the total taxes paid by the lowest income group and 67 per cent by the second lowest. Only from the fourth lowest income group upwards did the federal taxes begin to increasingly exceed the state and local taxes in the composition of taxes paid by different income groups.

[1] A recent study of distribution of the United States tax burden in 1966 revealed that when families were classified by selected percentiles in the income distribution, the tax rates also took on a U-shaped pattern: the tax rates rose in the very lowest and highest percentiles but remained essentially proportional for the vast majority of families. See Joseph Pechman and Benjamin A. Okner: Who bears the tax burden? (Washington, The Brookings Institution, 1974), pp. 50-52.

[2] In the Harriot-Miller study the incidence assumptions for the property tax were: (a) for owner-occupied non-farm dwellings, all paid by owners; (b) for tenant-occupied housing, all shifted to tenants; and (c) for non-residential property, all shifted to consumers. The assumptions made by the Brookings Institution are: (a) the tax on land is all paid by landowners; and (b) the tax on improvements is shifted to shelter and consumption.

[3] For a detailed discussion of the income concept used in the data provided by the Brookings Institution, see Joseph A. Pechman and Benjamin A. Okner: Who bears the tax burden? (Washington, The Brookings Institution, 1974), pp. 11-24.

Table III.4 Government Tax and Transfer Rates as a Percentage of Total Income in 1970

Class of adjusted family money income (in dollars)	Total			Federal taxes				State and local taxes		
	Taxes	Government transfer payments	Taxes minus transfer payments	Total	Income Tax	Corporate profit tax	Social security tax	Total	Property Tax	Sales Tax
Under 2,000	86.5	73.4	13.0	24.4	4.0	6.9	7.0	62.1	25.6	18.5
2,000-4,000	23.2	42.1	-18.9	7.7	1.3	1.7	2.8	15.5	7.1	5.5
4,000-6,000	21.7	31.6	- 9.9	9.7	2.3	1.6	4.0	12.0	5.4	5.1
6,000-8,000	23.5	18.6	4.9	12.9	3.9	1.6	5.4	10.6	4.5	5.1
8,000-10,000	25.2	10.4	14.7	15.1	5.5	1.6	6.2	10.0	4.1	4.8
10,000-15,000	25.5	5.2	20.3	16.2	6.6	1.4	6.4	9.3	3.7	4.4
15,000-25,000	25.6	2.7	22.9	17.1	8.3	1.6	5.6	8.5	3.3	3.7
25,000-50,000	26.1	1.3	24.7	18.2	10.6	2.2	4.0	7.8	3.1	2.9
50,000 and over	32.6	0.5	32.0	24.3	15.1	7.4	1.1	8.3	3.6	1.6
All income levels	26.3	5.7	20.6	17.3	8.5	2.3	4.8	9.0	3.7	3.7

Note: The income concept used includes government transfer payments. The assumptions used regarding the incidence of taxes are as follows:
Social security tax: federal, 3/4 shifted to wages and 1/4 to consumers; state and local, all shifted to wages.
Corporate profit tax: 2/3 shifted to stockholders and 1/3 to consumers.
Sales tax: all shifted to consumers.
Property tax: (a) the tax on land, all shifted to landowners; and (b) the tax on improvements, all shifted to shelter and consumption.

Source: Tax rates and transfer rates were computed from data on adjusted family income, taxes and government transfer payments in absolute amounts supplied to the ILO by The Brookings Institution.

While similar estimates are not readily available, the overall tax burden on the poor during the 1970s has probably not been reduced.

Favourable treatment of the rich

While the lowest income groups bear the heaviest tax burden, the upper income groups and corporations are known to have received favourable or preferential tax treatment in many different ways under the federal tax law. A systematic analysis of this complex and intricate subject is beyond this study. Some of its more obvious features may nevertheless be briefly indicated.

1. The capital gains preference

In the United States only one-half of the realised capital gain on an asset held over six months (defined as a long-term capital gain) has been included in taxable income. With the exclusion of the other half of the realised capital gain, effective federal income tax rates on most long-term capital gains during the 1970s ranged from 7 per cent to 35 per cent while other kinds of income and short-term capital gains were taxed at rates of 14 to 70 per cent.[1] The benefit of this preferential tax treatment went primarily to the upper income groups. According to a US Treasury analysis, in 1971 the capital gains preference for individuals cost the Treasury $5.6 billion. A further estimate revealed that less than 1 per cent of the nation's taxpayers with reported incomes of $50,000 and over received 70 per cent of these tax benefits ($3.9 billion) while 80 per cent of the taxpayers with reported incomes of $15,000 and under received less than 10 per cent of these tax benefits; and that in the $50,000 and over group the average amount of tax benefits received from capital gains was $8,000 per tax return compared to $11 per tax return in the $15,000 and under group. In the Treasury study presented during the 1969 tax reform hearing, it was pointed out that the half-tax on capital gains was "the most important factor in reducing the tax rates of those with high incomes". The Treasury study showed that capital gains reduced effective tax rates from 55.5 per cent to 32.7 per cent for those in adjusted gross income brackets of $1 million and over, in contrast to a consequent reduction from 16.4 to 16.2 per cent of the effective tax rates in the $5,000 to $10,000 brackets.[2]

The accumulation of capital gains has been a driving force in the concentration of wealth. Since only realised capital gains were taxable, investors who held on to their assets could increase

---

[1] George F. Break and Joseph A. Pechman: Federal Tax Reform: The Impossible Dream?, op. cit., pp. 44-45.

[2] Unless otherwise indicated, the material in this paragraph was drawn from Arnold Canter: "The Slippery Road to Tax Justice", in the American Federation of Labour and Congress of Industrial Organisations: AFL-CIO Federationist (Washington,D.C.) Apr. 1973, p. 4.

their wealth by the full amount of any accured capital gains without paying taxes. "Moreover, all capital gains accrued on assets transferred at the death of the owner are exempt from income tax, and those that are transferred by gift are subject to tax only if the receiver sells them before his death."[1] These were parts of the mechanism for concentration of wealth in the upper income groups. According to one estimate, between 1948 and 1964 capital gains accrued at an average rate of $40 billion a year.[2] This was more than twice the rate at which families saved all other kinds of income during the same period. As an indication of the high concentration of this kind of wealth, over 50 per cent of all capital gains accruing between 1960 and 1964 was estimated to have gone to the top 2 per cent of all income receivers (those with income of $25,000 or more) in 1962, compared to 11 per cent of the total ordinary income they received in that year. The latest data indicated that in 1972 tax returns reporting incomes of $25,000 or more accounted for 62 per cent of the capital gains and only 17 per cent of ordinary income.[3]

2. The insignificance of estate and gift taxes[4]

Estate and gift taxes are a fiscal instrument for preventing or reducing the concentration of wealth. These taxes assumed an insignificant role in the tax system of the United States as in those of other developed countries (see table III.2). As of 1975, under federal tax aw the exemptions were $60,000 for the estate tax and $3,000 a year for each donee plus a lifetime exclusion of $30,000 under the gift tax. The tax rates were high: estate tax rates reached a maximum of 77 per cent and for gift taxes the maximum was 57.75 per cent. But these rates applied to only a small fraction of the total property transfers between generations. Less than a quarter of the total wealth owned by those who died in any one year is estimated to have been subject to the estate and gift taxes. In fiscal year 1976 these taxes were expected to form only about 1.5 per cent of the tax revenue of the Federal Government.

The ineffectiveness of the estate and gift taxes is due to their structural defects. The transfer of accured capital gains at the death of the owner without the need to pay any income tax, as noted above, might be cited as one example. The major problem of these taxes, however, was their evasion by the rich through various legally permissible devices. One such device commonly in practice and most difficult to deal with is the use of trusts to transfer property from one generation to another. "For example, a man might set up a trust to pay out the income from his property to his wife for her life and then to the children for their lives;

---

[1] George F. Break and Joseph A. Pechman: Federal Tax Reform: The Impossible Dream?, op. cit., p. 45.

[2] Some 60 per cent of those capital gains accrued on corporate stock, 27 per cent on non-farm residential real estate, and 13 per cent farm real estate (ibid., p. 45).

[3] George F. Break and Joseph A. Pechman, op. cit., p. 45.

[4] Material on estate and gift taxes in this section was drawn from George F. Break and Joseph A. Pechman, op. cit., pp. 110-116.

at the death of the children the trust would be dissolved and the property distributed to the grandchildren. The property would be subject to estate tax when it was set up but there would be no tax when one of the income beneficiaries succeeded another or when it was terminated."[1]

While the distribution of wealth in a given year can be ascribed to a variety of factors, the lack of effective taxation on inheritance has been a basic factor making possible a high concentration of wealth in a relatively small number of families. Accurate data on wealth distribution in the United States is lacking. However, as a result of recent research efforts devoted to this difficult subject, a rough approximate picture of the concentration of wealth in the United States in 1970 has begun to emerge: the top 1 per cent of adult US wealth holders owned roughly 25 per cent of all personal property and financial assets.[2] The top 5 per cent of US family units held over 40 per cent of all wealth and the top 20 per cent had 75 per cent of all wealth; whereas the bottom 50 per cent of families accounted for only 3 per cent of all wealth.[3] It may be further noted that the size distribution of wealth was more unequal than the size distribution of personal income. As an indication, the top 10 per cent of families drew 29 per cent of total personal income but owned 56 per cent of all wealth, whereas the bottom 10 per cent of families drew 1 per cent of total personal income and owed more than they earned. The estimates cited here are probably subject to a wide margin of error. Nevertheless, they tend to indicate a high degree of inequality in the distribution of wealth.[4]

3. Tax exemption on interest from state and local government bonds[5]

This provision of the federal income tax law had provided a federal subsidy to state and local governments by enabling them to sell bonds at a lower interest rate. Individual ownership of state and local bonds has been highly concentrated in the upper income groups where the tax advantage was the greatest. Most other state and local bonds are owned by commercial banks and by non-life insurance companies. The shares of these financial institutions are mainly held by upper income groups. Thus, it is the upper income group which reaps directly or indirectly the tax benefits from exemption of state and local bond interest. In the

---

[1] George F. Break and Joseph A. Pechman, op. cit., p. 113.

[2] Estimate made by James D. Smith of Pennsylvania State University.

[3] Estimate made by Lewis Mandell, study director, based on data collected through interviews with 2,100 persons by the University of Michigan's Survey Research Centre.

[4] All the estimates of the distribution of wealth cited in this paragraph were taken from an article entitled "Who has the wealth in America?" published in Business Week (Highstown, New Jersey), 5 Aug. 1972, pp. 54-56. This article has assembled findings from recent studies on the distribution of wealth in the United States and produced a chart giving the Lorenz curves of the distribution of wealth in 1970 and of the distribution of income in 1969 for purposes of comparison.

[5] Unless otherwise stated, material for this section was drawn from George F. Break and Joseph A. Pechman, op. cit., pp. 52-54.

1969 Treasury study referred to above it was observed that tax-free income from state and local bonds was the second most important factor - second to capital gains - in reducing the taxes of those with incomes of over $100,000 per year.[1]

4. Income splitting[2]

The income-splitting provision was adopted by Congress in 1948 with the object of extending the privilege of income splitting for tax purposes. One special feature of this provision was that married couples filing separate returns were required to use the old single person income tax rate schedule, whose tax brackets were half as wide as the brackets for couples filing joint returns. Thus, the effect was to double the width of the tax brackets and thereby reduce progression in the tax rates and tax liabilities. The tax advantage was greater for married couples with one earner than for two-earner families. But because of progressivity of the federal income tax, the tax benefit from income splitting increased with increase in taxable income. It has been shown that under the tax rates prevailing in 1975 the tax benefit rose from a mere $5 for married couples with taxable income of $1,000 to as much as $14,510 for couples with taxable income of $200,000 or more. The revenue loss amounted to no less than about $32 billion a year.

5. Tax privileges of corporations

Under the federal tax law tax privileges of various kinds have been granted to corporations. Among the more widely discussed ones were accelerated depreciation, investment credit, mineral industry subsidies, tax deferrals for activities with immediate capital costs but with little or no immediate return and inadequacy of the minimum tax on selected tax preference income items concerning corporations. In addition, special tax privileges had been accorded to American transnational corporations with subsidiaries in foreign countries. One such privilege was tax deferral, which permitted US corporations to pay no income tax on the profits of foreign subsidiaries until such profits were brought back home, and substantial amounts of these profits were reinvested abroad and did not come home. Another privilege was the foreign tax credit, under which income taxes paid by subsidiaries to foreign governments were deducted dollar for dollar from the parent corporation's US income tax liability when a portion of the subsidiaries' profits was brought back to the United States. Still another tax privilege, designed to stimulate exports, was tax deferral for domestic international sales corporations (DISCs) set up by domestic manufacturers to handle the export of their products.

As a result of these and other tax privileges, a large discrepancy was created between the nominal federal tax rate and the effective tax rate of corporation income tax. In 1975, for all

---

[1] This statement was cited in Arnold Cantor: "The Slippery Road to Tax Justice", in AFL-CIO Federationist, Apr. 1973, loc. cit., p. 4.

[2] The material for this section was drawn from George F. Break and Joseph A. Pechman, op. cit., p. 32.

large corporations the nominal tax rate was 48 per cent, but the effective tax rate, measured in relation to true economic income, was little more than 35 per cent.[1] This explains, in part, the low share of corporation income tax in the total federal tax revenue, amounting to about 16 per cent in 1973, as shown in table III.1. The low tax burden on corporations means the transfer of an increasing tax burden on to individuals and, in particular, the low and middle income groups. The tax benefits reaped by corporations were mostly passed on to upper income groups either in the form of increased dividends they received or in the form of capital gains on corporate stocks they owned.

The foregoing analysis has brought out certain basic irrationalities of the whole fiscal system from the point of view of income distribution. First, while the low income groups received public income maintenance benefits, the upper income groups received tax benefits. Though estimates were not available, the total amount of tax benefits reaped by the upper income groups from the fiscal system is likely to have exceeded the total amount of public assistance benefits paid to the lowest income groups.

Second, the benefits paid to the recipients, poor and non-poor, under social insurance - the main pillar of income maintenance - were, in fact, paid primarily out of low wages of the working poor and near-poor and the earned incomes of wage and salary earners whose wages or salaries were below the ceiling on payroll tax which was $15,300 in 1976. Unearned incomes from property and higher earned incomes beyond the ceiling played no part in this redistribution process.

Third, the lowest income groups have borne the heaviest tax burden. Except for the federal income tax, they paid the highest tax rate for all the major taxes. One striking irrationality in this connection was that the government transfer payments received by the lowest income groups were offset to a large extent by the high taxes they paid.

Finally, the lack of effective taxation on inheritance had led to a high concentration of wealth in a relatively small number of rich families. The latter, together with the large tax benefits they received had, in turn, generated a high degree of inequality in the size distribution of personal incomes.

These irrationalities point to the need for a reform of the tax system which would have to cover not only federal taxes but state and local ones as well.

Proposals for tax reform

Tax reform in the United States is generally regarded as a most complicated and intricate subject. Only seasoned tax experts know about it. Moreover, the tax laws have been under continuous revision and reform. The latest tax reform act was adopted by

---

[1] George F. Break and Joseph A. Pechman, op. cit., p. 91.

Congress in the later part of 1976. At the time of writing (March 1977) the new Carter administration was about to initiate a thorough investigation into the whole matter on the basis of which a new tax reform bill will be prepared and put before Congress.

The purpose of this section is to present several options for tax reform emanating from outside the Government. The proposed reform options have been put forward recently by two outstanding tax experts, Joseph A. Pechman and George F. Break. It should be noted that the options deal with the federal tax system only.

The Pechman-Break proposal[1]

The Pechman-Break proposal contains four alternative reform packages or reform options which yield the same revenue as the present law by different combinations of different revisions of specific taxes. "The objectives emphasised in these packages are, first, improvement of the progressivity of the federal tax system and, second, reduction of marginal income taxes applying to additions to individual income. Although seemingly contradictory, these objectives can be reconciled by broadening the income tax base to include items of income that are not now taxed or are given preferential rates and to eliminate unnecessary personal deductions."[2]

The four reform packages or options presented in their proposal "range from fairly modest changes that would leave the present system basically the same, to drastic revisions that would fundamentally alter the taxation of labour and capital income".[3] The revisions introduced are confined to the three major taxes in the federal tax system: the individual income tax, the corporation income tax and the payroll taxes. Table III.5 gives a summary of structural revisions under four reform options. Tables III.6 and III.7 present effective federal rates of individual and corporation income and payroll taxes under present law and under four reform options respectively, by comprehensive income class, 1976, and by population decile, 1976.

It is not proposed to enter into a discussion of the numerous structural revisions of the three major federal taxes summarised in table III.5.

---

[1] For detailed discussion of their tax reform proposal, see George F. Break and Joseph A. Pechman: Federal Tax Reform: The Impossible Dream?, op. cit., in particular Chapter 6: "Alternative Reform Packages", pp. 121-135.

[2] ibid., p. 121.

[3] ibid., p. 122.

Table III.5

Summary of Structural Revisions under Four Reform Options

Item	Option A	Option B	Option C	Option D
Capital gains				
Increase holding period from six months to one year	X	a	a	a
Eliminate alternative tax	X	a	a	a
Tax capital gains as ordinary income	...	X	X	X
Constructive realisation of capital gains	X	X	X	X
Tax on preference income				
Reduce $30,000 exemption to $5,000	X	a	a	a
Eliminate deduction for taxes	X	a	a	a
Raise tax rates to one-half the ordinary rates (present base)	X	a	a	a
Personal deductions				
Eliminate state gasoline tax deduction	...	X	X	X
Eliminate separate health insurance premium deduction	...	X	X	X
Raise medical expense floor from 3 to 5 per cent	...	X	X	X
Eliminate property tax deduction	...	X	X	X
Limit interest deduction to property and business income plus $2,000	...	X	X	X
Repeal percentage standard deduction and raise low-income allowance to $3,000	...	X	X	X
Treatment of married couples and single people				
Remove rate advantages of income splitting	...	X	X	X
Provide 10 per cent tax credit (up to $1,000) for spouse with lower earnings	...	X	X	X

Item	Option A	Option B	Option C	Option D
Other provisions				
Eliminate percentage depletion	X	X	X	X
Eliminate deferral through DISCs	...	X	X	X
Eliminate deferral of income of foreign-controlled corporations	...	X	X	X
Eliminate dividend exclusion	...	X	X	X
Eliminate maximum tax on earned income	...	X	X	X
Repeal tax on preference income	...	X	X	X
Payroll tax				
Introduce $900 per capita exemption and $2,000 low-income allowance, with phase-out of $1 for every $2 of earnings (employee and self-employed only)	X	...	...	...
Introduce $900 per capita exemption and $2,000 low-income allowance; eliminate ceiling on maximum taxable earnings; raise tax rate by 1.7 percentage points (employee, employer and self-employed)	...	X	X	X
Integration				
Tax all corporate earnings to shareholders at individual income tax rates[b]	...	...	X	X

[a] Revision not relevant because capital gains would be taxed in full.

[b] Tax-exempt organisations are assumed not taxed on their allocated share of corporate earnings.

Source: George F. Break and Joseph A. Pechman: Federal Rax Reform: The Impossible Dream? (The Brookings Institution, Washington D.C., 1975), p. 128.

Table III.6

Effective Federal Rates of Individual and Corporation Income and Payroll Taxes under Present Law and under Four Reform Options, by Comprehensive Income Class, 1976

Income classes in thousands of dollars; other numbers in percent

Comprehensive income class[a]	Present law	Option A	Option B	Option C	Option D
0-5	11.3	8.2	3.8	3.6	3.1
5-10	18.2	16.4	12.3	12.7	11.6
10-15	21.4	20.6	16.7	17.3	16.1
15-20	22.9	22.9	20.6	21.6	20.2
20-25	23.6	23.6	24.0	25.0	23.5
25-50	25.2	25.3	30.7	31.2	30.0
50-100	31.9	32.8	41.0	39.1	41.8
100-200	36.0	39.4	45.7	42.7	50.4
200-500	39.3	44.8	48.7	44.5	55.7
500-1,000	42.1	49.4	51.2	45.4	58.6
1,000 and over	41.9	52.1	51.9	44.5	58.3
All classes[b]	24.0	24.0	24.0	24.0	24.0

[a] Includes adjusted gross income, the share of corporate retained earnings and the corporate tax allocated to individuals, half of total estimated capital gains transferred by gift or death, excess of percentage depletion over cost depletion, and interest on state and local government bonds.

[b] Includes negative incomes not shown separately.

Sources:

Brookings 1970 tax file, projected to 1976. The options are explained in the text.

George F. Break and Joseph A. Pechman, op. cit., p. 126.

Table III.7

Effective Federal Rates of Individual and Corporation Income and Payroll Taxes under Present Law and under Four Reform Options, by Population Decile, 1976, Percent

Population decile[a]		Present law	Option A	Option B	Option C	Option D
First	($ 3 400)	10.6	6.3	1.5	1.1	0.8
Second	($ 6 350)	13.6	11.6	7.7	7.8	6.9
Third	($ 9 300)	18.5	16.7	12.4	12.8	11.7
Fourth	($12 300)	20.6	19.3	15.4	15.9	14.7
Fifth	($15 150)	22.0	21.5	17.7	18.4	17.1
Sixth	($18 000)	22.7	22.7	20.0	21.0	19.6
Seventh	($21 850)	23.4	23.4	22.3	23.4	21.9
Eighth	($25,650)	23.9	23.9	25.1	26.0	24.4
Ninth	($32 950)	24.5	24.6	28.8	29.4	27.9
Tenth		32.5	34.9	41.3	39.2	43.6
All deciles[b]		24.0	24.0	24.0	24.0	24.0

[a] Population deciles are in order of comprehensive income ranked from low to high. Figures in parentheses are the top income limits of the deciles, which are based on the distribution of all single persons and families by size of income. The 1976 limits were obtained by extrapolation from 1966 on the basis of the increase in national income per capita. Data for 1966 are from Joseph A. Pechman and Benjamin A. Okner, Who Bears the Tax Burden? (Brookings Institution, 1974).

[b] Includes negative incomes not shown separately.

Sources: Brookings 1970 tax file, projected to 1976.

George F. Break and Joseph A. Pechman, op. cit., p. 127.

Some observations will be made, however, on the differences in effective federal rates of the three major taxes under the four reform options compared with those under the federal tax in effect for calendar year 1975. The tax liabilities for 1976 under the individual and corporation income taxes and the payroll tax were estimated to be $260 billion, or 24 per cent of the income of all those filing tax returns. The income concept used here approximates a comprehensive definition of income. All the four reform options were designed in such a way as to yield the same tax liabilities of $260 billion and the same effective federate rate of 24 per cent of income for all classes in 1976. Each option, however, embodies a different pattern of structural revision such that the progressivity of the effective federal rates increases successively from Option A to Option D.

As can be seen from table III.6, for the lowest income class in the bracket of 0-$5,000, while the effective federal rate in 1975 of the three taxes was 11.3 per cent, under Option A the effective rate would be reduced to 8.2 per cent and fall to 3.1 per cent under Option D. The reductions of effective rate in this lowest income class are explained almost entirely by progressive revisions of the payroll tax. At the upper end for the income class of $1 million and over compared with the 1975 effective rate of 41.9 per cent, the effective rate would be increased to 52.1 per cent under Option A and to 58.3 per cent under Option D.

Of a greater interest is the progressivity of the federal tax rate arranged according to population deciles. Here the rises in progressivity are most striking with respect to the first and second decile. For the first decile compared with a 10.6 per cent effective rate under the1975 tax law, Option A decreases it to 6.3 per cent but only from Option B onwards is the effective rate drastically reduced to 1.1 per cent under Option C and to 0.8 per cent under Option D. A similar pattern of progressivity can be discerned for the second decile: Option A yields a very moderate decrease in the effective rate (from 13.6 per cent under the present law to 11.6 per cent), whereas Options B, C and D decrease it to 7.7, 7.8 and finally 6.9 per cent or to half of the 1975 effective rates. As regards the tenth decile, for which Option A raises the effective rate moderately from the 1975 rate of 32.5 per cent to 34.9 per cent, Option D increases it substantially to 43.6 per cent.

After having briefly reviewed both the AFL-CIO tax loophole-closing programme and the four Pechman-Break tax reform options, two general remarks may be made on the direct impact of these two proposals on poverty alleviation. First, as mentioned previously, both proposals are concerned exclusively with federal tax reform. Measures for removing the heavy tax burden on the poor imposed by state and local taxes seem to be equally important; and these still remain to be considered. Second, the recapturing by the Federal Government of tax benefits granted to upper income groups proposed by the AFO-CIO programme may not, by itself, have any favourable impact on the poor unless complementary measures are taken to direct the use of the recaptured tax benefits to the improvement of the life of the poor. As regards the Pechman-Break tax reform options, it would seem that even under Option D the impact on the first and second population decile would be very limited. For the first decile, whose upper income limit was $3,400 in 1976, even a complete elimination of the 10.6 per cent under the 1975 federal tax law would add only a maximum of $347 to their annual income, and those in the first decile would still live much below the poverty line. For the second population decile whose upper income limit was $6,350, a deduction of the effective federal rate from 13.6 per cent under the 1975 federal tax law to 6.9 per cent under Option D would add a maximum of $425 to their income or an increase of no more than 6.7 per cent. The impact would be rather small.

Thus, from the point of view of anti-poverty policy, in addition to tax reform such as those envisaged in the proposals reviewed above, some other direct measures for poverty alleviation would be required. Among such measures, negative income tax proposals have been put forward. These proposals will be considered in the following section.

Negative income tax plans

Seeing the need for a universal (as opposed to a specific approach to the alleviation of poverty), there has been growing advocacy of a federal guaranteed minimum income for all. Negative income tax plans are an outgrowth of this conception. This section begins with a short discussion of the general concept of a negative income tax scheme. A brief comparison will then be made of several earlier negative income plans to demonstrate that under the general concept, a negative income tax plan can be designed differently to serve different specific objectives. Following this comparison, the plan of income maintenance reform recommended by the Joint Economic Committee's Subcommittee on Fiscal Policy of the US Congress in 1974 will be analysed in greater detail,[1] since this plan - also known as the Griffiths plan - was not only the latest and the most comprehensive negative income tax plan considered in the United States at the time of writing (March 1977), but also had been introduced in both Houses of Congress for deliberation and congressional action.

The general concept of a negative income tax scheme

The concept of a negative income tax is very simple. It originates in the unfairness of treatment of low income earners in the federal income tax law. While for those whose incomes are high enough to be liable for income tax receive tax exemptions and

---

[1] See 93rd US Congress, 2nd Session: Joint Economic Committee: Income Security for Americans: Recommendations of the Public Welfare Study: Report of the Subcommittee on Fiscal Policy of the Joint Economic Committee, 5 Dec. 1974, Ch. VIII to Ch. XI, pp. 155-237; and 93rd US Congress, 2nd Session: Joint Economic Committee: Paper No. 16, A Model Income Supplement Bill: A Staff Study prepared for the use of the Subcommittee on Fiscal Policy of the Joint Committee, 20 Dec. 1974 (Washington, 1974).

deductions which reduce their taxable income by the same amount. Thus, they can enjoy a tax saving which would be considerable for those in the upper income brackets because of progressivity of marginal income tax rates. Low income earners whose incomes are below the level of tax exemptions plus deductions, on the other hand, receive no similar favourable treatment aside from paying no income tax. Out of this sense of unfairness it has been proposed that an income supplement be provided to those whose incomes are below that level. Thus conceived, the income tax system would consist of two parts: those with incomes more than the sum of exemptions plus deductions would pay to the Government a positive income tax and those earning less than this or with no income would receive from the Government a negative income tax, that is, an income supplement.

The simplicity of this concept provides scope for a wide variety of negative income tax (NIT) plans proposed since the early 1960s as a measure for poverty alleviation in the United States. Each has its own specific objectives and characteristics. Nevertheless, all these plans contain three common policy variables, namely a federal guaranteed minimum income for families or individuals with no other income, a tax rate on earned income (or a benefit reduction rate) and a break-even income. The three policy variables are inter-related in such a way that any one of the three is jointly determined by the other two.[1] What is important to note are the conflicting effects of these variables on (a) poverty reduction; (b) budget cost; and (c) work incentives. A higher guaranteed minimum income would raise the population in poverty closer to the poverty line or minimum living standard, but many policy makers believe that this would impair the work incentives of the employable poor. To preserve work incentives, the designers of NIT plans generally set the tax rate on earned income at much less than 100 per cent and often at 50 per cent.[2] But the higher the federal guaranteed minimum income and the lower the tax rate on income, the higher will be the break-even income and consequently the greater will be the cost to the federal budget. The different kinds of NIT plans proposed are largely the outcome of these conflicting policy considerations.[3]

---

[1] In Algebraic terms the relationships of these policy variables can be expressed as follows: let G denote the guaranteed minimum income, t the tax rate on earned income and B the break-even income. In addition, let Y denote the recipient's earned income and S the amount of income supplement paid to the recipient. Then

$$G = tB, \quad t = \frac{G}{B}, \quad B = \frac{G}{t}; \quad \text{and}$$

$$S = G - tY = t(B - Y).$$

[2] There is, in fact, not much precise emperical knowledge in this complex field of work response. A recent well-designed negative income tax experiment conducted in four cities in New Jersey and one city in Pennsylvania tested eight combinations of guaranteed income level and tax rate on income (guaranteed income level as 50 per cent, 75 per cent, 100 per cent and 125 per cent of the poverty line combined with a tax rate on income of 30 per cent, 50 per cent and 70 per cent). The finding of this experiment was that there were no major differences in work behaviour between the families in the experimental group and those in the control group who received no negative tax payments. See David N. Kershaw: "A negative-income-tax experiment", in Scientific American (New York), Oct. 1972, p. 23.

(Footnote 3 on p. 137.)

A comparison of selected NIT plans

Seven NIT plans have been selected for purposes of comparison. These are listed as follows:[1]

1. Friedman plan.[2]

2. Lampman negative rates plan.

3. Family Assistance Plan (FAP) of the Nixon Administration.

4. Heineman Commission Plan.

5. Yale plan.

6. Rolph plan.

7. Griffiths plan.

Broadly, these seven NIT plans fall into three groups. Their major differences are indicated briefly below.

(Footnote 3 from p. 136.)

[3] For a detailed discussion of various types of NIT plans and technical problems involved in their design, see, in particular, Organisation for Economic Co-operation and Development: Negative income tax (Paris, 1974), and Christopher Green: Negative taxes and the poverty problem (Washington, The Brookings Institution, 1967).

[1] Except for the Friedman plan and the Griffiths plan, the other five NIT plans are reproduced in Theodore R. Marmor (ed.): Poverty Policy: A Compendium of Cash Transfer Proposals (Chicago, Aldine-Atherton, 1971). The original sources of these five plans are as follows:

The Lampman negative rates plan: Robert J. Lampman: "Expanding the American system of transfers to do more for the poor", in Wisconsin Law Review (Madison), 1969, No. 2, reproduced in Marmor, op. cit., pp. 108-116.

The FAP plan: Summary of Family Assistance Act of 1969 in Marmor, op. cit., pp. 97-98 and Statement of Secretary of Health, Education and Welfare, Robert H. Finch in explanation of the Family Assistance Act 1969, in Marmor, op. cit., p. 91.

The Heineman Commission plan: Extract from Poverty amid Plenty: The American Paradox, Report of the President's Commission on Income Maintenance Programs (also known as Report of the Heineman Commission, after the Commission's Chairman, Ben W. Heineman) (Washington 1969), reproduced in Marmor, op. cit., pp. 183-203.

The Yale plan: James G. Speth, Jr., Richard Cotton, Joseph C. Bell and Howard V. Mindus: "A model negative incomx tax statute", in Yale Law Journal (New Haven, Connecticut), Vol. 78, 1969, reproduced in Marmor, op. cit., pp. 126-188.

The Rolph plan: Earl R. Rolph: "The case for a negative income tax device", in Industrial Relations (Berkeley, California), Feb. 1967, in Marmor, op. cit., pp. 207-217.

(Footnote 2 on p. 138.)

The first group comprises the Friedman plan, Lampman negative rates plan and the Nixon Family Assistance Plan (FAP). One common characteristic of these three plans is the very low levels of guaranteed minimum incomes - set at 25 to 50 per cent of the poverty line. But each has its specific purpose and envisages a different relationship with public assistance. The Friedman plan, while the first of its kind, is, in fact, the most stringent of all. The plan aims to use negative income tax to replace public assistance, but the benefits it brings to the poor are far lower than the prevailing benefits from public assistance.[1] For the Lampman negative rates plan, the specific purpose is to supplement public assistance programmes by providing a federal cash allowance to families of the working poor excluded from specific public assistance.[2] The Family Assistance Plan was designed primarily to replace the much criticised AFDC by a federal income supplement paid to families with children and to extend coverage to the fully employed male working poor with children. When combined with the accompanying Food Stamp Proposal, the guaranteed minimum incomes are appreciably higher than those given in the Family Assistance Plan alone. Both the Lampman plan and the FAP place strong emphasis on work incentives for the working poor, the former deliberately setting the cash allowance far below the subsistence level and the latter including a work requirement provision for able-bodied persons.

The second group covers the Heineman Commission plan and the Yale plan. In contradistinction to the limited-objective NIT plans described above, these two plans are aimed at the eradication of poverty and the replacement of public assistance. The Heineman Commission plan sets as the goal the lifting of all the population in poverty up to the poverty line by means of a universal negative income tax system. However, for budgetary purposes and with a view to prompt implementation, the initial programme recommended by the Commission provides a basic guarantee level that is still below the poverty line. The initial programme would replace public assistance completely in states with low payment levels and partially in those with higher levels. It may be added that neither the Heineman Commission plan nor the Yale plan contains a work requirement provision.

(Footnote 2 from p. 137.)

[2] See Milton Friedman: Capitalism and freedom (Chicago University Press, 1962), pp. 190-195.

[1] In commenting on the Friedman plan, one writer has observed that: "Viewed either as an over-all average or as a minimum guaranteed income where there is no other income, the rate of subsidy would have fallen far short of the amounts forthcoming under existing categorical assistance programs - an academic way of saying that substitution of Friedman's plan for public assistance to 7.8 million on assistance would have been a literal disaster to them." (George H. Hildebrand: Poverty, Income and the Negative Income Tax (Ithaca, New York, Cornell University, 1967), p. 26.

[2] This would be introduced in the second stage of Lampman's two-stage plan, the first calling for the adoption of federal standards raising assistance benefits to $1,500 in all states for four-person families in the traditional public assistance categories and with no income.

The Yale plan adopts a bolder approach than the Heineman Commission plan. It proposes to raise the federal guaranteed minimum income at once to the poverty line, which each family and individual may claim as a matter of right. Another interesting feature of this plan is its provision for the integration of negative income tax with positive income tax in the over-all income tax system. A family which elects to receive income supplement will be subject to a special tax of 50 per cent on its other income comprehensively defined. The family will also pay a federal income tax, but these payments are deductible in such a manner that the combined effect of the two taxes will not exceed the special tax of 50 per cent. Table III.8 shows the relationship between the positive and negative income tax programme for a family of four under the Yale plan. It will be seen that at a before-tax income of $6,400 a "break-even point" will be reached when the total tax liability ($3,200) equals the basic income supplement. But above this point some net negative income tax transfer will still remain which can be used to partially offset the positive income tax liability. Only when the before-tax income has increased to $7,916 will the "tax break-even point" be reached (i.e. the net negative income tax is zero).

A third group of NIT plans is represented by the Rolph plan and the Griffiths plan. These two plans differ from the other NIT plans in the basic design by introducing into their respective plans a universal tax credit or a universal tax credit and income-tested grants. By such fiscal devices the negative income plan provides at the same time a mechanism for income redistribution. The Griffiths plan will be analysed later. Here attention will be drawn to two basic features of the Rolph plan: (a) a system of flat-sum credits to which all the population would be entitled and (b) a general proportional income tax with zero exemptions. The net tax liability of a person or a family, positive or negative, can be computed from the following formula:

$$T = rY - uC$$

where T denotes the net tax liability, Y the taxable income, r the tax rate, C the size of the credit (assuming uniform per capita credits) and u the number of credits for the unit (normally the family). A proportional income tax combined with a tax credit can be converted into a progressive tax. Table III.9 gives an illustration of the working of such a plan for a family of four assuming a tax rate of 30 per cent and a credit of $500 per person. Under these assumptions, a family of four within the income range from zero to slightly in excess of $6,000 would receive a net payment at a diminishing rate, while those with an income above this level would pay tax at an increasing rate. By raising the tax rate, for instance, to 50 per cent, the upper income limit (or the break-even point) for receiving a net payment of credits will be cut down to $4,000.

To facilitate further comparison the working of the Lampman negative rates plan, Friedman plan, Family Assistance Plan and Heineman plan for a family of four with their respective guaranteed minimum income level, marginal tax rate on income, break-even point and some other relevant data are brought together in table III.10. Chart II depicts a comparative picture of the relation between family income before tax and allowances, and family income after tax and allowances as incomes increase starting from zero for a family of four under the six NIT plans discussed above and identifies for each plan its locus on the break-even line.[1]

(Footnote 1 on p. 141.)

Table III.8

The Yale Negative Income Tax Plan for a Family of Four

($)

a Family income before tax	b Positive tax liability	c Negative tax liability $\left(\frac{a-2b}{2}\right)$	d Total tax liability (b+c)	e Basic income supplement	f Net government transfer (e-d)	g Net NIT transfer (e-c)	h Family income after tax (a+f)
0	0	0	0	3 200	3 200	3 200	3 200
1 000	0	500	500	3 200	2 700	2 700	3 700
3 000	4	1 496	1 500	3 200	1 700	1 704	4 700
6 000	450	2 550	3 000	3 200	200	650	6 200
6 400	511	2 689	3 200	3 200	0	511	6 400
7 000	603	2 897	3 500	3 200	-300	303	6 700
7 916	758	3 200	3 958	3 200	-758	0	7 158

Source: Speth, Cotton, Bell and Mindus, in Marmor, op. cit. p. 166.

Table III.9

The Credit Income Tax: an Illustration[1]

($)

Income	Net tax	Disposable income
0	-2 000	2 000
1 000	-1 700	2 700
2 000	-1 400	3 400
4 000	-800	4 800
6 000	-200	6 200
8 000	+400	7 600
10 000	+1 000	9 000
20 000	+4 000	16 000
50 000	+13 000	37 000
100 000	+28 000	72 000
1 000 000	+298 000	702 000

[1] The table assumes a tax rate of 30 per cent and credits of $500 a person for a family of four.

Source: Rolph, in Marmor, op. cit., p. 214.

In this comparative perspective the Yale plan is the only one that fulfils the objective of eliminating poverty by the official definition, but the budget cost it requires, estimated roughly at $27 billion, is considered probably too high to be politically acceptable. A striking feature of the Yale plan, as clearly shown in Chart II, is that by far the larger part of the cost will be spent on the non-poor. This can be traced to the 50 per cent tax rate which combines with the poverty line as the guaranteed minimum income to move its break-even point to $6,400 (twice the poverty line income), practically the highest along the line. To a lesser extent the same can be said about the Heineman Commission plan. That large numbers of the non-poor would benefit from these plans could perhaps be looked upon from two different points of view. If the objective is exclusively to move people above the official poverty line, then this would be treated as a "spill-over" effect of preserving work incentives. If, on the other hand, the objective is to improve income distribution with respect to, say, the first quartile of the population, the "spill-over" effect may be precisely what the NIT plan is aimed at. This appears to underlie the Rolph plan with its built-in mechanism for income redistribution, even though the size of credit and the 30 per cent tax rate chosen in this plan are merely for purposes of illustration.

Among the other three plans, the Friedman plan, as already explained, could do harm to the poor. The Lampman negative rates plan and the Family Assistance Plan, though their costs are relatively low, are only partial NIT plans, with no universal coverage and, furthermore, are attached to rather severe work incentive provisions. The two plans are calculated to narrow the poverty gap but are not expected to lift many people above the poverty line.

The Griffiths plan

The Griffiths plan, proposed to begin in 1977 and under consideration by both Houses of Congress, is not only the latest but also the most comprehensive negative income tax plan ever produced in the United States.

Its main purposes are to overhaul the entire income maintenance system by making the Federal Government assume full responsibility for financing and managing the system, by universal coverage and standardisation of benefits throughout the country and also to establish a direct link between income maintenance and federal income tax.

The plan contains three key elements which are briefly described below:

(Footnote 1 from p. 139.)

[1] Family incomes after taxes and allowances are plotted only up to the break-even line because beyond this line a negative income tax plan will have no more effect and the disposable family incomes, which will be below this line, will be determined by the schedule of positive income tax which it is not proposed to enter in this chart.

Table III.10

Income and Net Benefit per Year for a Family of Four Under Lampman Negative Rates Plan, Friedman Plan, Family Assistance Plan and Heineman Commission Plan

($)

	Net benefit				Total income			
Family income before benefit	Lampman negative rates plan	Friedman plan	Family Assistance Plan[1]	Heineman plan	Lampman negative rates plan	Friedman plan	Family Assistance Plan	Heine-man plan
0	750	1 500[2]	1 600	2 400[3]	750	1 500	1 600	2 400
500	750	1 250	1 600	2 150	1 250	1 750	2 100	2 650
1 000	750	1 000	1 460	1 900	1 750	2 000	2 460	2 900
1 500	750	750	1 210	1 650	2 250	2 250	2 710	3 150
2 000	500	500	960	1 400	2 500	2 500	2 960	3 400
2 500	250	250	710	1 150	2 750	2 750	3 210	3 650
3 000	0	0	460	900	3 000	3 000	3 460	3 900
3 500	0	0	210	650	3 500	3 500	3 710	4 150
4 000	0	0	0	400	4 000	4 000	4 000	4 400
5 000	0	0	0	0	5 000	5 000	5 000	5 000
Guaranteed minimum income as % of poverty line income	25	50	46	62				
Marginal tax rate on income (%)	50[4]	50	50[5]	50				
Poverty-line income	3 000	3 000	3 500[6]	3 900[7]				
Break-even income	3 000	3 000	3 920	4 800				
Estimated net cost of the plan ($'000 million)	4	.[8]	4[9]	6				

[1] $500 for each of the first two members of a family plus $300 for each additional member. [2] One-half of $3,000 of income tax exemptions plus standard deductions (= $600 exemption for each person plus $300 for the family head and $100 for each dependant). [3] $750 per adult and $450 per child. [4] Marginal tax rate is zero up to $1,500 and 50 per cent above $1,500. [5] With an earned income disregard (allowance) of $720. [6] Poverty-line income in 1968. [7] Projected poverty line for 1971. [8] No cost estimate. [9] Including $600 million for job training and child care centres.

Sources: For the first three plans see citations in the text. For the Heineman Commission Plan see extracts from *Poverty amid plenty: The American Parodox*, in Marmor, op. cit., pp. 183-203.

Chart II. Effects on the Poor of Alternative Negative Income Tax Plans.

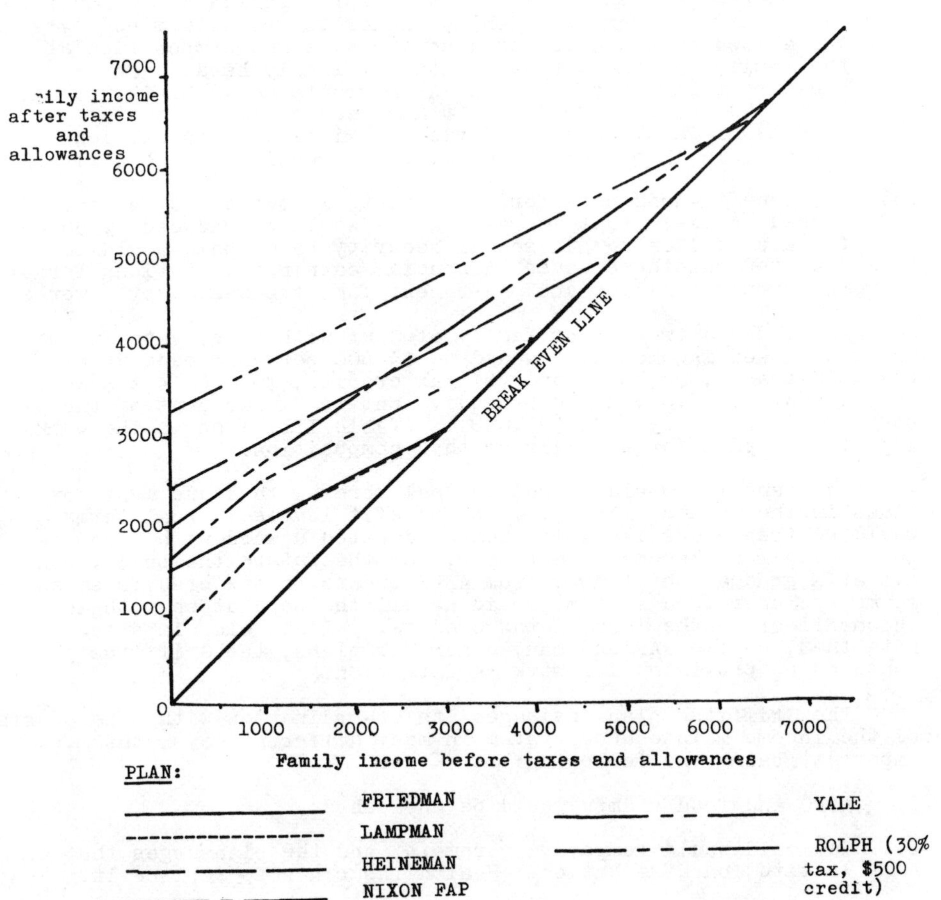

PLAN:

FRIEDMAN
LAMPMAN
HEINEMAN
NIXON FAP
YALE
ROLPH (30% tax, $500 credit)

(1) A universal annual tax credit of $225 per person against income tax liability. This calls for the following corresponding changes in the Federal Income Tax Law proposed in the plan: (a) elimination of personal exemption and low-income deduction; (b) a moderate reduction of the federal income tax rate at the break-even point to remove the "notch effect"; and (c) administration of the plan by the Internal Revenue Service (IRS).

(2) Income-tested cash grants for the poor labelled Allowance for Basic Living Expenses (ABLE). Benefits are determined by the allowance schedule based on the size and composition of the family and the marital status of family head. For a two-parent family of four the ABLE grants would be $2,700 (= $2,050 + $325 + $325). It has been estimated that 11 million families and individuals, including 34 million persons, in 1976 would be eligible to receive ABLE benefits.

(3) The benefit-loss rate for ABLE grants is set at 50 per cent for earned income; that is, allowances would be reduced by 50 cents for each dollar. But social security taxes paid would be deducted and there would be special earnings deductions for two-earner families and one-parent families headed by a worker.

Thus, for a two-parent family of four with no private income the guaranteed income floor would be $3,600 per year made up of (a) ABLE grants, $2,700; and (b) tax credits, $900 (= 4 x $225). This amount of $3,600 would be equivalent to 71 per cent of the poverty line in July 1974 ($5,058). Table III.11 shows the working of this plan for a family of this composition.

The benefits would be set in real terms with adjustment for rises in the cost of living. The benefit levels in real terms would be treated as flexible, to be adjusted upward with rises in per capita real income. Moreover, for the future the policy would aim at a gradual shift away from ABLE grants to tax credits so as to move closer to a system providing all the population with an income floor in the form of tax credits. It is also important to note that, unlike FAP and many other NIT plans, the Griffiths plan contains no provision for work registration.

The Griffiths plan envisages its co-ordination with other parts of the income maintenance system in many different ways, the more important being the following:

1. AFDC and food stamps would be abolished.

2. Medicaid would temporarily remain, and the plan urges the institution of a National Health Insurance to replace it.

3. Public housing would not be phased out because the housing programme is not sufficiently dispersed. Housing subsidy would be counted as income for determination of ABLE benefits.

4. State supplementation to ensure no loss to AFDC recipients in states where AFDC benefits exceed ABLE benefits under the Griffiths plan.

5. Exclusion from the plan of participants in the federal SSI programme.

Table III.11

Benefits and Taxes for a Father, Mother and 2 Children at Varying Earnings Levels Under the Subcommittee Plan

Annual earnings	Federal income tax liability[1]	Tax credits	Net federal income tax liability[2]	Social security tax	ABLE grant	Net cash income[4]
$	$	$	$	$	$	$
0	0	900	+900	0	2 700	3 600
500	0	900	+900	29	2 464	3 835
1 000	0	900	+900	58	2 229	4 071
1 500	0	900	+900	88	1 994	4 306
2 000	0	900	+900	117	1 758	4 541
2 500	0	900	+900	146	1 523	4 777
3 000	0	900	+900	176	1 288	5 012
4 000	0	900	+900	234	817	5 483
5 000	0	900	+900	292	346	5 954
6 000	124[3]	900	+776	351	0	6 425
7 000	595[3]	900	+305	410	0	6 895
8 000	1 066[3]	900	166	468	0	7 366
9 000	1 314	900	414	526	0	8 060
10 000	1 490	900	590	585	0	8 825
15 000	2 510	900	1 610	772	0	12 618
20 000	3 820	900	2 920	772	0	16 308
25 000	5 340	900	4 400	772	0	19 788

[1] Based on the standard deduction but with no low-income allowance. Personal exemptions are replaced by $225 per person tax credits.

[2] Numbers with plus signs indicate net payments to, rather than from, taxpayers, because of tax credits.

[3] Tax is a reduced amount from regular schedule because of provision for smooth transition from ABLE recipient to non-recipient status.

[4] Assuming no state supplementation, social security taxes, using the current tax rate and taxable wage bases, are deductable from earnings in computing ABLE grants.

Source: 93rd US Congress, 2nd Session, Joint Economic Committee: *Income Security for Americans: Recommendations of the Public Welfare Study*, op. cit., p. 172.

As regards the probable effects of the plan, it has been estimated that the plan would almost halve the poverty gap in 1976 from $19.3 billion to $10.4 billion, and the number of families and individuals in poverty would fall from 11.9 to 9.4 million. It was pointed out that these calculations used a poverty measure based on disposable (or after-tax) income. The plan has made it clear that it was not designed to be tied to the poorest who are to receive public aid on a case-by-case basis. The benefits of the plan are designed to supplement work incomes of the working poor, formerly excluded from specific programmes, and also the incomes of moderate wage earners. Furthermore, the plan would provide minimum disincentive effects to work and minimum incentives to family splitting and non-marriage.

Unlike most other NIT plans, the Griffiths plan would produce a redistribution effect from the introduction of tax credit and the elimination of personal tax exemption. While personal tax exemption at $750 per person would be of little interest to those with little or no taxable income, it would be worth as much as $525 to the high-income taxpayers. The plan has estimated that "for most tax-paying families of four with annual income below $25,000, the $225 credit would cut income taxes. For many other taxpayers income taxes would rise by varying amounts".[1] Some examples of such cases are shown in table III.12.

The net full-year cost of the plan (estimated for fiscal year 1976) to the Federal Government is estimated to be $15.4 billion, which is almost equally divided between income taxes foregone for low and middle-income taxpayers and additional benefits to low-income units.

From the foregoing analysis it can be seen that the Griffiths plan, which emerges as a compromise of conflicting objectives, has brought basic changes into the existing income maintenance system through a unified approach embodied in the form of an innovative negative income tax plan characterised by a combination of universal tax credits and income-tested grants.

---

[1] 93rd US Congress, 2nd Session: Joint Economic Committee: Income Security for Americans: Recommendations of the Public Welfare Study, op. cit., p. 156.

Table III.12

After-tax Income Under Current Law and Under Subcommittee Plan for 4-person Families at Different Earnings Levels: Families of 2 Parents and 2 Children: 1 Parent Works Full time

	A		B		C		D	
	Current	Proposed	Current	Proposed	Current	Proposed	Current	Proposed
Earnings	0	0	$3 000	$3 000	$5 000	$5 000	$7 500	$7 500
Allowances	.[1]	$2 700	.[1]	2 700	.[1]	2 700	.[1]	2 700
Offset income[2]	.[1]	0	.[1]	1 500	.[1]	2 500	.[1]	2 700[3]
ABLE payments	.[1]	2 700	.[1]	1 200	.[1]	200	.[1]	0
Tax liability[4]	0	0	0	0	98	0	484	1 050[3]
Credits	...	900	...	900	...	900	...	900
Net tax	0	(900)[5]	0	(900)[5]	98	(900)[5]	484	150
Net income	.[1]	3 600	3 000[1]	5 100	4 902[1]	6 100	7 016[1]	7 350
Gain (or loss)	...	+3 600[1]	...	+2 100[1]	...	+1 198[1]	...	+334[1]

	E		F		G		H	
	Current	Proposed	Current	Proposed	Current	Proposed	Current	Proposed
Earnings	$10 000	$10 000	$15 000	$15 000	$25 000	$25 000	$50 000	$50 000
Allowances	10 000	10 000	...	2 700	...	2 700	...	2 700
Offset income[2]	...	2 700[3]	...	2 700[3]	...	2 700[3]	...	2 700[3]
ABLE payments	...	0	...	0	...	0	...	0
Tax liability[4]	905	1 490	1 820	2 510	4 380	5 340	14 560	16 060
Credits	...	900	...	900	...	900	...	900
Net tax	905	590	1 820	1 610	4 380	4 440	14 560	15 160
Net income	9 095	9 410	13 180	13 390	20 620	20 560	35 440	34 840
Gain (or loss)	...	+315	...	+210	...	-60	...	-600

(Footnotes 1 to 5 on p. 148.)

(Footnotes 1 to 5 from p. 147.)

[1] Family might be eligible for AFDC or food stamps under current law, but amount would vary based on a number of factors.

[2] Earnings offset allowances by 50 cents for each $1. Not shown is the deduction from earnings of social security taxes permitted under the allowance system.

[3] Fifty per cent of earned income exceeds gross allowances, so only that portion of income which completely offsets allowances is shown here. Thus, no ABLE payment is received. For family D, the excess offset income is $1,050 ($3,750-$2,700), which is less than the regular income tax liability of $1,071. Thus, family D would substitute the smaller amount, against which credits are then applied.

[4] Standard deduction of 15 per cent up to $2,000 is assumed. A family with income of $50,000 undoubtedly would itemise deductions and pay less tax.

[5] Numbers in parentheses indicate net payments to, rather than from, taxpayers, because of tax credits.

Source: 93rd US Congress, 2nd Session: Joint Economic Committee: Income Security for Americans: Recommendations of the Public Welfare Study, op. cit., p. 170.

Chapter 4

Conclusions

Poverty in perspective

In analysing poverty in the United States or in any other country, it is important to draw a distinction between poverty before and after public transfer payments. Pre-transfer poverty arises from causes rooted in the economic and social conditions of the country, whereas post-transfer poverty can be reduced by increased public income transfers. The latter, however, deal mainly with the symptoms of pre-transfer poverty but not its causes.

Between 1960 and 1975, measured by a commonly used relative poverty standard (i.e. one-half of the median family income) post-transfer poverty showed practically no decline in the United States. It, however, did decline markedly, measured by the official absolute standard (i.e. the official poverty line).

The size of post-transfer poverty is the difference between the size of the pre-transfer poverty and the extent of poverty reduction brought about by public income transfers. In this study an attempt was made to ascertain the relative importance of these two factors in determining the movement of the trend in post-transfer poverty measured by the official poverty line over the whole period from 1960 to 1975. One difficulty encountered is the lack of yearly time series data on pre-transfer poverty in the United States which it would be highly useful for policy making to collect and publish along with the annual statistics on post-transfer poverty. From limited available data on pre-transfer poverty and other relevant material the broad findings are as follows.

The steep downward post-transfer poverty trend up to the mid-1960s was due primarily to the decline in pre-transfer poverty caused by the improved employment situation resulting from rapid economic expansion. Public income transfers played a minor role; the amount of public transfers during that period, though on the increase, was still relatively moderate.[1]

Since the mid-1960s the relative role of the two factors has completely changed. The pre-transfer poverty trend started to rise slowly during the second half of the 1960s and the early 1970s due to (a) the slackening of economic growth and (b) a pronounced

---

[1] Robert J. Lampman observed: "The increases in money transfers have been largely directed at the pre-transfer non-poor. Of course, the number of people counted as poor has declined dramatically - from 23 per cent of the population in 1959 to 12 per cent in 1968 - but that is apparently due primarily to rising wage rates and improved employment opportunities for low-income people. The unemployment rate fell from a post-war high of 6.8 per cent in 1959 to below 4 per cent in 1966 ..." (See Robert J. Lampman: "The Transfer Approach to Distribution Policy" in The American Economic Review, May 1970, Papers and Proceedings of the Eighty-second Annual Meeting of the American Economic Association, New York, 28-30 Dec. 1969, p. 275.)

combined increase in pre-transfer poor families with children headed by non-aged women and in pre-transfer poor unrelated individuals - combined increase exceeding the decrease in pre-transfer poor families with children headed by non-aged males. Then came the 1974-75 severe recession during which the rising trend in pre-transfer poverty moved sharply upwards if only because of the large increases in the unemployed.

On the other hand, since the mid-1960s the trend in income transfers was rapidly rising concurrently with the rising trend in pre-transfer poverty. The rapid increases in income transfers can be traced to the successive growth of different types of income transfer programmes: first, the explosion of AFDC, then the improvements in social security, the expansion of food stamp programmes and medicaid followed by the great increases in unemployment compensation during the 1974-75 recession. Against this perspective of rising trends both in pre-transfer poverty and in income transfers significant reductions in post-transfer poverty since the mid-1960s could only be accounted for by income transfers increasing at a faster rate and in far greater size than the decreases in pre-transfer incomes of poor households.

The causes of pre-transfer poverty

The level of pre-transfer poverty in the United States has been relatively high. In fiscal year 1976 about one out of every four families (including unrelated individuals as single-person families) would have had pre-tax money incomes below the official poverty line in the absence of any public transfer payment. Families with the highest pre-transfer poverty incidence were headed by non-Whites (43.7 per cent), by aged persons (59.9 per cent), and single person families (49.5 per cent). Among female-headed families with children the pre-transfer poverty incidence is also known to be very high. Significantly, of all families headed by persons under 65 years of age, no less than 18.7 per cent lived in pre-transfer poverty.[1]

The high pre-transfer poverty incidence was a manifestation of inequalities in the size distribution of primary personal income attributed in part to a high concentration of wealth. In fiscal year 1976, whereas the top 20 per cent of families received 50.2 per cent of the total pre-tax/pre-transfer income, the poorest 20 per cent received as little as 0.3 per cent and the second poorest 20 per cent only 7.2 per cent.[2]

---

[1] Figures for pre-transfer poverty incidence are from the Congress of the United States, Congressional Budget Office: Poverty Status of Families Under Alternative Definitions of Income, op. cit., pp. 25-31.

[2] Congress of the United States, Congressional Budget Office: Poverty Status of Families Under Alternative Definitions of Income, op. cit., p. 24.

Most of the heads of pre-transfer poor families had a low educational attainment and low acquired marketable skills. The jobs available to them were unskilled or semi-skilled jobs. These jobs generally paid low wages due partly to their lack of effective unionisation and consequent weak bargaining power and partly due to an excess supply of low-skilled labour relative to demand. With the low wages they earned, the heads of families were usually unable to lift their families above poverty without supplementary income from a second earner in the family. Even though many of the low wage earners during their working life managed to live above the poverty line, once they became aged and withdrew from the labour market, they would be among the poorest of the pre-transfer poor because they had little or no past savings to draw upon.

Lack of job opportunities for unskilled and semi-skilled workers was another cause of their living in pre-transfer poverty. The unemployment rate among these workers was always much higher than among skilled workers. In addition to the wholly unemployed, large numbers of them were able to find only part-time employment throughout the year and many others could only obtain seasonal jobs. As a long-term trend technological changes in the United States economy have entailed a continuous relative decrease in the demand for unskilled and semi-skilled labour. At a slow rate of economic growth the surplus labour in this broad category tended to increase. This was accentuated by an increasing proportion of the growing labour force being women and youths with a low level of acquired skills. With regard to women, a significant number of them were heads of families with young children. They were unable to work outside the home in the absence of adequate day care services.

For the pre-transfer poor there were, furthermore, barriers to their upward mobility along the incomes scale. First, there was, in varying degrees, an inter-generational transmission of poverty. The incidence of poverty varied inversely with the level of educational attainment. In this respect, the children of poor people were in many ways disadvantaged from the very start. For instance, even though high school was free, many of them did not complete high school because they had to take up an unskilled job as a second earner, or even as the sole earner in the family.

A second barrier to their upward mobility was racial and sex discrimination. In the educational system there was discrimination against non-Whites, one major example being school segregation between White and Black children. Discriminatory practice also prevailed in employment in the form of stratified labour markets. Where educational attainment was equal, the wages and earnings for non-Whites were generally lower than for Whites and those for females lower than for males. Non-Whites and females were usually assigned to jobs paying low wages and were, by and large, not given the same opportunity to move up to high-paying jobs through on-the-job training, upgrading and promotion as their White and male counterparts. As a result of federal action discrimination both in education and in employment had been reduced but they continued to exist.

Shortcomings of the existing income transfer system

The causes of pre-transfer poverty such as those mentioned above would have to be removed by measures other than public income transfers. None the less, the income transfer policy of the United States since the mid-1960s did produce a powerful direct impact on poverty alleviation. As a result of large increases in public transfers, the level of post-transfer poverty measured by the official poverty line has fallen considerably over the past decade.

Despite its impressive record of success, the existing income transfer policy, however, contains a number of serious shortcomings, which were examined in this study. These are recapitulated below.

To begin with, the existing official poverty standard is not a standard based on relative poverty which, as many have advocated, could serve as a guide to income transfer policies aimed at reducing the proportion of population at the low end of the income distribution. It is an absolute poverty standard based on a fixed minimum level of consumption established in the early 1960s by the official poverty line (converted into money income and adjusted for subsequent changes in the cost of living) for families of different size and composition. Even as an absolute standard, the "basic needs" covered by the official poverty line constitute no more than a "minimum subsistence standard". This standard has been criticised as being far too low in relation to the average American living standard, especially as the latter had been rising over the past decade. Therefore, a higher poverty standard is needed not only as a yardstick for counting the poor but as a basis for income transfer policy or other anti-poverty policy.

Turning to the over-all income transfer system in existence, the present study has drawn attention to its two major shortcomings. First, it has shown the gross inequalities arising from the relation of income transfers to taxation in the fiscal system. These can be attributed to the following features:

1. The lowest income groups bore the relatively heaviest tax burden. The transfer payments they received were largely offset, or even exceeded, by heavy taxes they paid.

2. The benefits under social insurance paid to the poor and non-poor were financed primarily by a payroll tax levied on wages and salaries up to a taxable ceiling. Thus, the payroll tax was highly regressive. Moreover, except for the self-employed, incomes from property (such as dividends) were not subject to the payroll tax.

3. The upper income groups reaped an enormous sum in tax benefits which probably exceeded the total amount of welfare benefits received by the lowest income groups. According to a US Treasury Study prepared for the Senate Budget Committee, in fiscal year 1977 while $28 billion of tax benefits went to corporations, tax benefits for individuals amounted to no less than $84 billion, almost half of which went to persons with incomes of $30,000 a year or more or to about 5 per cent of all taxpayers.[1]

[1] Figures released to the press and reported in the International Herald Tribune (Paris), 14 Feb. 1978, p. 3.

4. Lack of effective taxation on inheritance has led to the concentration of wealth, which together with tax benefits, in turn generated inequality in the size distribution of personal income.

Second, although the working of the income transfer system had greatly reduced the over-all magnitude of post-transfer poverty, wide differences in post-transfer poverty incidence persisted among subgroups of the poverty population. The incidence remained markedly higher for non-Whites than for Whites, for female-headed families than for male-headed families, and for unrelated individuals than for persons living in families. While these differences originated in the differences in pre-transfer poverty incidence between the subgroups, they could be narrowed or eliminated by improving the income transfer system.

The over-all income transfer system is composed of two parts: social insurance, of which the largest programmes are old-age, survivors, disability and medicare for the aged (OASDHI) and unemployment insurance; and income assistance under which the largest cash assistance programmes are Aid to Families with Dependent Children (AFDC) and Supplemental Security Income (SSI) for the aged, disabled or blind, and the largest in-kind assistance programmes are medicaid and food stamps. Social insurance, which is based on the contributory principle, requires no means or income test. Its benefits are wage-related and are paid to the poor and non-poor alike. Income assistance programmes, on the other hand, are means or income-tested and are designed specifically for improving the income position of the poor.

Though not targeted on the poverty population, social insurance has made a far greater impact on the over-all reduction in poverty than income assistance. For the aged the dramatic decline of post-transfer poverty incidence from the exceedingly high pre-transfer incidence was due mostly to the great improvements in old-age pension combined with medicare for the aged. Other social insurance programmes have reduced substantially poverty among the non-aged. Since it covers the non-poor as well as the poor, public expenditure on social insurance in 1977 was 2.5 times as large as that on income assistance.[1]

---

[1] In 1977 the total public expenditure on major income transfer programmes amounted to $183 billion of which $134.2 billion was allotted to social insurance and $49.3 billion to income assistance. The breakdown of each division is given below:

Major social insurance programmes		Major income assistance programmes	
Programme	1977 expenditure (billions)	Programme	1977 expenditure (billions)
Old age - survivors insurance	$71.0	Aid to Families with Dependent Children	$10.3
Unemployment insurance	14.3	Supplemental Security Income	6.3
Medicare	21.0	Medicaid	17.2
Disability insurance	10.9	Food stamps	5.0
Workmen's compensation	6.7	General assistance	1.3
Veterans' compensation	5.7	Housing assistance	3.0
Railroad retirement	3.6	Veteran's pensions	3.1
Black	1.0	Earned income tax credit	1.3
		Basic opportunity grants	1.8
Sub-total	$134.2	Sub-total	$49.3

Source: Budget of the United States Government, Fiscal Year 1978, 17 Jan. 1977.

While social insurance is well developed in the United States and has an indispensable role to play in poverty alleviation, it raises various problems, some of which can be briefly indicated. First, the benefits being mostly wage-related, the lowest paid workers usually received the least benefits even though the minimum social security benefits have been significantly increased. This explains why social insurance contributed much less to poverty reduction among non-Whites than among Whites. Secondly, for a variety of reasons including inflation to which the social security benefits are adjusted and a perspective rising proportion of the aged in the population, the financing of social security payments is becoming increasingly difficult both in the short and longer run. The existing payroll tax is found to be inadequate to meet the increasing demands on social security. The payroll tax rate would have to be raised with further increases in the tax burden of low wage earners unless resort could be made to other methods of financing, e.g. abolition of the taxable ceiling and financing the additional demands from general revenue.

The income assistance programmes, which together form what has been called the welfare system (within the over-all income transfer system), have been subjected to far more severe criticism than social insurance. The existing welfare system is not an integrated system. It is an outcome of piece-meal and unco-ordinated growth of separate programmes in response to different needs and pressures over the past decades. It has some shortcomings which are summarised below.

1. Categorisation of the poor. Under the existing welfare system the poor households are treated with a varying degree of favour according to the "employability" of the poor. The most favoured are the aged, the disabled and the blind who are entitled to a federally financed and administered SSI which makes up for the unduly low social security benefits or non-entitlement to such benefits and which provide for them a nationally uniform cash income floor. The less favoured are poor families with dependents headed by women who are eligible for AFDC or, less frequently, those headed by unemployed fathers who are eligible for AFDC-UF. The least favoured are the working poor - non-aged working male family heads with dependent children, non-aged childless couples and non-aged unrelated individuals. The poor households in this least favoured category are not eligible for income assistance programmes open to the more favoured categories except for general assistance and food stamps even though the earnings from their work are very low and lower than the benefits received by many households in the other categories.

2. Wide inter-state disparities. Nearly all the state administered welfare programmes financed partly or wholly from state and local funds display wide differences in eligibility requirements and benefit levels. Generally, in the poor states in the South where the poverty incidence is high and where a large proportion of the Black poverty population is located the benefit levels are much much lower than in the rich states. The striking instances are AFDC and Medicaid. Similarly, the differences in the level of unemployment benefits, which belong in social insurance, also needs to be mentioned. The inter-state disparities can be ascribed basically to the inadequacy of the financial and administrative machinery used which, in turn, can be traced to the state-federal relations in the structure of the existing welfare system.

3. Low cash benefits. Under the cash assistance programmes the level of cash benefits was set quite low. For AFDC, notwithstanding its wide inter-state variations, in none of the 53 states in 1974 was the maximum payment for a penniless mother with three children above the poverty line, while in 14 states it was between 70 and 50 per cent of the poverty line, and in 17 states it was 50 per cent below. When the maximum AFDC payment was combined with allowable food stamp bonus, the combined payment exceeded the poverty line only in 3 states, and in 27 states it was still less than 80 per cent of the poverty line.[1] Even for the aged the guaranteed national cash income floor set for a couple by SSI in 1974 was still 12 per cent below the poverty line.[2]

4. The side effects of multiple-benefits arrangements. The recipients of benefits from cash assistance programmes wholly or partially financed by the Federal Government such as SSI, AFDC or AFDC-UF are automatically eligible for benefits from in-kind assistance programmes - food stamp bonus, medicaid and housing assistance. The multiple-benefits arrangements have contributed greatly to raising their low levels of living, since the benefits from individual cash assistance programmes, as noted above, were set very low. But these arrangements have engendered certain serious side effects. First, as explained in this study, they have unwittingly built into the welfare system disincentives to the recipients to work or to work for a higher earned income because of (a) an exceedingly high cumulative benefit reduction rate implicit in these arrangements and (b) the "notch effect" on their income especially with respect to the loss of medicaid at a certain level of earned income. Second, in many households without earned incomes the amount of the combined benefits they received from different assistance programmes, in cash and in kind, was, in fact, greater than the earnings of a full-time worker, working for a low wage. This phenomenon of "leap-frogging" not only created vertical inequity but provided financial incentives for low-wage male family heads to leave home in order to enable their families to qualify for AFDC and other benefits.

5. The inequality of medicaid. As a quantitative assessment has shown, medicare for the aged and medicaid for the non-aged had a far greater impact on reducing the over-all magnitude of poverty than all other in-kind transfer programmes combined. Yet, in regard to the existing medicaid, its defects have proved to be much more serious than other income assistance programmes. Apart from its income notch effect on work incentives referred to above, the distribution of medicaid was strikingly inequitable. The eligibility for medicaid is restricted to certain categories of the non-aged poor. In consequence, faced with the frightfully high hospitalisation and medical expenses, those excluded from medicaid and not covered by company health insurance schemes - mostly families headed by male working poor and non-aged unrelated individuals - live in perpetual fear of financial disaster caused by sickness. What is more, the regional differences in medicaid

---

[1] See Supra, table II.7.

[2] The income floor set by SSI for an aged couple in July 1974 was $219 per month or $2,628 per year and the poverty line for a non-farm aged couple in 1974 was $2,982.

benefits are so great that those received by the poor in the South are only a small fraction of those received by the poor in the Northeast. Since adequate medicaid is a vital need of all the poor and since the morbidity rate among the poor is particularly high, the reform of medicaid or its replacement by a national health insurance geared to the special needs of the low-income population is clearly of capital importance for raising the well-being of the poor. Among other in-kind assistance programmes the inequities and limited coverage of housing assistance under the various federal housing programmes needs to be stressed and much remains to be done to meet adequately the housing needs of the poverty population.

6. The leakage of income assistance expenditures to the non-poor. While social insurance benefits were paid to both poor and non-poor as a matter of principle, expenditure on income assistance, though designed specifically for poverty alleviation, was, to a lesser extent, also distributed to the non-poor owing to the rules of eligibility for several programmes and fraud. It may, however, be noted that many of the non-poor who benefited from income assistance had pre-transfer incomes only moderately above the poverty line; by a higher poverty standard they might as well be counted as poor.

7. Work requirements without adequate job opportunities. For the "employable" poor their eligibility requirements for income assistance usually include work requirement provisions. Employable recipients of AFDC are required to register for training and employment under the Work Incentive Programme. For eligibility for the food stamp programme non-aged able-bodied recipients must also register to work. These work requirement provisions proved to be rather ineffective. The main reason was because adequate job opportunities were not available more especially for those whose acquired skills were low and who much exceeded market demand. The training services provided were insufficient in quantity and left much to be desired in quality. Moreover, a large proportion of AFDC mothers had to look after their young children and could not work outside the home without low-cost but adequate day care.

8. Administrative complexity. As the present study has shown, the administration of the welfare system in the United States was extremely complex. The complexity stemmed partly from the uncoordinated growth of different programmes but partly from a divided responsibility of the Federal, state and local governments for financing, legislating and managing different programmes within this system. This has resulted in a loss in efficiency and in a lack of unified national effort to attain certain clearly defined national goals in anti-poverty policy.

9. Stigma. To be a recipient of income assistance or welfare benefits one had to go through the means or income test. The passing of the means test was a stigma - a label of being poor. People generally detested it. Moreover, the recipients, especially AFDC mothers, were subjected to close checking and supervision by the case workers which often encroached upon the privacy of the recipients.

10. Perpetuation of an inordinate "relief-receiving" dependent social class. Lastly, an improvement of the incomes of the pre-transfer poor through the income assistance or welfare system does not alter the underlying fact that the poor lack earned income or the incomes they earn are so very low that they cannot break out of

poverty. Increasing their incomes by means of an income subsidy simply means that they depend on government support to make their ends meet. This puts them in a state of dependency. For taxpayers welfare benefits are, in essence, money spent on poor relief; hence they are preoccupied with its possible negative effect on work incentive. What needs emphasis is the importance of removing the causes of pre-transfer poverty. If the Government relied primarily on the income assistance or welfare approach for poverty alleviation with little effective action for eliminating pre-transfer poverty, there is a likelihood of perpetuating an inordinate "relief-receiving", dependent socio-economic class in American society.

Future policy

Eradicating pre-transfer poverty calls for longer term measures which the Government has been taking with increased vigour since the war-on-poverty launched in 1964. It is beyond the scope of this study to enter a discussion of such measures. In the short-run there is an imperative need for overhauling the existing welfare system, as can be seen from its various shortcomings indicated above. A recent document prepared by the US Department of Health, Education and Welfare, reviews several options for welfare reform discussed by a Consulting Group in 1977.[1] It might be fitting to end this chapter by a review of the best of these options.

To commence with, two general observations may be made. First, all options for welfare reform accept the low official poverty line; none of them proposes a higher and more socially desirable poverty standard. Second, no mention is made of the vital importance of reforming medicaid and there is more obvious general ignorance of the need for reform of housing assistance.

Of all proposals that have been put forth for welfare reform, the one titled the "triple-track strategy" (TTS) appears to be much better designed both from the analytical and operational points of view. Under the approach the poverty population is viewed as falling into three groups, each requiring a special assistance strategy:

[1] Organisation for Economic Co-operation and Development: Working Party on Social Aspects of Income Transfer Policy: Recent Proposals for the Reform of the US Welfare System, document submitted by the US Department of Health, Education and Welfare to the Working Party for Information (Document No. MAS/WO4(77)9, Paris, 12 Oct. 1977), mimeographed.

Poverty population group	Assistance strategy
1. Households which contain an employed adult but which have insufficient earnings to meet basic consumption needs.	An expanded earned income tax credit and food stamps.
2. Households in which an adult is expected to work but has no job.	Training and placement assistance, food stamps and, for some, a public service job. Those awaiting placement would receive a special unemployment assistance benefit.
3. Households in which no adult is expected to work outside the home.	Federal cash benefit equal to 75 per cent for the poverty line.

In addition, Supplemental Security Income (SSI) would be retained.

It will be recalled that Chapter 2 concluded with a list of desirable properties of any reform of the welfare system, and the TTS can be analysed on the basis of these properties. While little has been said about the budgetary implications of the strategy, its proponents believe that the clarification of budgetary responsibility should lead to a more efficient system with obvious ramifications on cost. And although it does not appear that there is a great simplification in the system in terms of the number of programmes, the afore-mentioned clarification of responsibility would tend to refocus the tasks of various government departments both on welfare and employment assistance lines.

The TTS contains components which meet all the other desirable properties of welfare reform. Although not clearly specified concerning the particulars, use is made of an expanded income tax credit for the working poor. If properly designed and substantially increased, this could result both in a marginal decrease in benefits as income increases and have a significant impact on disposable income. Secondly, the TTS removes inequities due to inter-state disparities by federalisation of nearly all welfare programmes. Finally, this approach places a great deal of emphasis on training and employment for the unemployed poor and, consequently, is aimed at solving the major underlying cause of pre-transfer poverty. The TTS appears to be the most commendable approach to welfare reform but many of the ambiguities, e.g. how much of an increase in the earned income tax credit, what special provisions will be made for youth unemployed or those seasonally unemployed, will need to be specified in much greater detail before the approach can be translated into specific action programmes.

Concluding comments

While welfare programmes and their reform will remain burning questions in the political arena of the US, the most important aspect of any programme will be ways in which the causes of poverty can be attacked. Welfare programmes are interventions which treat the symptoms and, unless properly designed, will not remove the causes. The major cause of poverty is the fact that the poor cannot find appropriate employment which emanates from the fact that they are either unsuitably trained or lack necessary skills. As a result, their earning capacity is dismally low. This has been compounded by the current welfare system which discourages self-improvement and employment by making them unprofitable in many cases. By most accounts, substantial progress was made over the decade 1965-75 in assuring minimal standards of food, housing, education, medical care and income.[1] Any major reform of the welfare system in the future will need to create the necessary conditions for those who are potentially employable to find productive and remunerative work while providing for the needs of those whose situation makes paid employment less appropriate. To emphasise freedom from want is no longer sufficient. It must be freedom for something, and that freedom is not safety but opportunity.

---

[1] Robert Haveman, ed., A Decade of Federal Antipoverty Programmes: Achievements, Failures and Lessons (New York, Academic Press, 1977).